some chinese ghosts

LAFCADIO HEARN

D1250275

DOVER PUBLICATIONS, INC.
Mineola, New York

Bibliographical Note

This Dover edition, first published in 2008, is an unabridged republication of the edition published by Little, Brown, and Company, Boston, in 1906. The first edition of the book was published in 1887.

Library of Congress Cataloging-in-Publication Data

Hearn, Lafcadio, 1850–1904.
    Some Chinese ghosts / Lafcadio Hearn.
      p. cm.
    "This Dover edition, first published in 2008, is an unabridged republication of the work published by Little, Brown, and Company, Boston, in 1906. The first edition of this book was published in 1887"—T.p. verso.
    ISBN-13: 978-0-486-46306-3
    ISBN-10: 0-486-46306-0
    1. China—Social life and customs—Fiction. 2. Legends—China. I. Title.

PS1917.S6 2008
813'.4—dc22

                                 2007051596

Manufactured in the United States of America
Dover Publications, Inc., 31 East 2nd Street, Mineola, N.Y. 11501

To my friend

HENRY EDWARD KREHBIEL

THE MUSICIAN

WHO, SPEAKING THE SPEECH OF MELODY UNTO THE

CHILDREN OF TIEN-HIA, —

UNTO THE WANDERING TSING-JIN, WHOSE SKINS

HAVE THE COLOR OF GOLD, —

MOVED THEM TO MAKE STRANGE SOUNDS UPON THE

SERPENT-BELLIED SAN-HIEN;

PERSUADED THEM TO PLAY FOR ME UPON THE

SHRIEKING YA-HIEN;

PREVAILED ON THEM TO SING ME A SONG OF THEIR

NATIVE LAND, —

THE SONG OF MOHLÍ-HWA,

THE SONG OF THE JASMINE-FLOWER

iii

If ye desire to witness prodigies and to behold marvels,
Be not concerned as to whether the mountains are distant
or the rivers far away.

KIN-KOU-KI-KOAN

Preface

I think that my best apology for the insignificant size of this volume is the very character of the material composing it. In preparing the legends I sought especially for *weird beauty;* and I could not forget this striking observation in Sir Walter Scott's "Essay on Imitations of the Ancient Ballad": "The supernatural, though appealing to certain powerful emotions very widely and deeply sown amongst the human race, is, nevertheless, a *spring which is peculiarly apt to lose its elasticity by being too much pressed upon."*

Those desirous to familiarize themselves with Chinese literature as a whole have had the way made smooth for them by the labors of linguists like Julien, Pavie, Rémusat, De Rosny, Schlegel, Legge, Hervey-Saint-Denys, Williams, Biot, Giles, Wylie, Beal, and many other Sinologists. To such great explorers, indeed, the realm of Cathayan story belongs by right of discovery and conquest; yet the humbler traveller who follows wonderingly after them into the vast and mysterious pleasure-grounds of Chinese fancy may surely be permitted to cull a few of the marvellous flowers there growing,—a self-luminous *hwa-wang*, a black lily, a phosphoric rose or two,—as souvenirs of his curious voyage.

L.H.

New Orleans, March 15, 1886.

Contents

*She hath spoken, and her words still resound
in his ears.*

HAO-KHIEOU-TCHOUAN: C. ix.

The Soul of the Great Bell

The water-clock marks the hour in the *Ta-chung
sz'*,—in the Tower of the Great Bell: now the mal-
let is lifted to smite the lips of the metal monster,—
the vast lips inscribed with Buddhist texts from the
sacred *Fa-hwa-King*, from the chapters of the holy
Ling-yen-King! Hear the great bell responding!—how
mighty her voice, though tongueless!—*KO-NGAI!* All
the little dragons on the high-tilted eaves of the green
roofs shiver to the tips of their gilded tails under that
deep wave of sound; all the porcelain gargoyles tremble on their carven perches; all the hundred little bells
of the pagodas quiver with desire to speak. *KO-NGAI!*
—all the green-and-gold tiles of the temple are vibrating; the wooden goldfish above them are writhing
against the sky; the uplifted finger of Fo shakes high
over the heads of the worshippers through the blue
fog of incense! *KO-NGAI!*—What a thunder tone was

1

that! All the lacquered goblins on the palace cornices wriggle their fire-colored tongues! And after each huge shock, how wondrous the multiple echo and the great golden moan and, at last, the sudden sibilant sobbing in the ears when the immense tone faints away in broken whispers of silver,—as though a woman should whisper, *"Hiai!"* Even so the great bell hath sounded every day for well-nigh five hundred years,—*Ko-Ngai:* first with stupendous clang, then with immeasurable moan of gold, then with silver murmuring of *"Hiai!"* And there is not a child in all the many-colored ways of the old Chinese city who does not know the story of the great bell,—who cannot tell you why the great bell says *Ko-Ngai* and *Hiai!*

Now, this is the story of the great bell in the Ta-chung sz', as the same is related in the *Pe-Hiao-Tou-Choue,* written by the learned Yu-Pao-Tchen, of the City of Kwang-tchau-fu.

Nearly five hundred years ago the Celestially August, the Son of Heaven, Yong-Lo, of the "Illustrious," or Ming, dynasty, commanded the worthy official Kouan-Yu that he should have a bell made of such size that the sound thereof might be heard for one hundred *li*. And he further ordained that the voice of the bell should be strengthened with brass, and deepened with gold, and sweetened with silver; and that the face and the great lips of it should be graven with blessed sayings from the sacred books, and that it should be suspended in the centre of the imperial capital, to sound through all the many-colored ways of the City of Pe-king.

Therefore the worthy mandarin Kouan-Yu assembled the master-moulders and the renowned bell-smiths of the empire, and all men of great repute and cunning in foundry work; and they measured the materials for the alloy, and treated them skilfully, and prepared the moulds, the fires, the instruments, and the monstrous melting-pot for fusing the metal. And they labored exceedingly, like giants,—neglecting only rest and sleep and the comforts of life; toiling both night and day in obedience to Kouan-Yu, and striving in all things to do the behest of the Son of Heaven.

But when the metal had been cast, and the earthen mould separated from the glowing casting, it was discovered that, despite their great labor and ceaseless care, the result was void of worth; for the metals had rebelled one against the other,—the gold had scorned alliance with the brass, the silver would not mingle with the molten iron. Therefore the moulds had to be once more prepared, and the fires rekindled, and the metal remelted, and all the work tediously and toilsomely repeated. The Son of Heaven heard, and was angry, but spake nothing.

A second time the bell was cast, and the result was even worse. Still the metals obstinately refused to blend one with the other; and there was no uniformity in the bell, and the sides of it were cracked and fissured, and the lips of it were slagged and split asunder; so that all the labor had to be repeated even a third time, to the great dismay of Kouan-Yu. And when the Son of Heaven heard these things, he was angrier than before; and sent his messenger to Kouan-Yu with a letter, written upon lemon-colored silk, and sealed with the seal of the Dragon, containing these words:—

"From the Mighty Yong-Lo, the Sublime Tait-Sung, the Celestial and August,—whose reign is called 'Ming,'—to Kouan-Yu the Fuh-yin: Twice thou hast betrayed the trust we have deigned graciously to place in thee; if thou fail a third time in fulfilling our command, thy head shall be severed from thy neck. Tremble, and obey!"

Now, Kouan-Yu had a daughter of dazzling loveliness, whose name—Ko-Ngai—was ever in the mouths of poets, and whose heart was even more beautiful than her face. Ko-Ngai loved her father with such love that she had refused a hundred worthy suitors rather than make his home desolate by her absence; and when she had seen the awful yellow missive, sealed with the Dragon-Seal, she fainted away with fear for her father's sake. And when her senses and her strength returned to her, she could not rest or sleep for thinking of her parent's danger, until she had secretly sold some of her jewels, and with the money so obtained had hastened to an astrologer, and paid him a great price to advise her by what means her father might be saved from the peril impending over him. So the astrologer made observations of the heavens, and marked the aspect of the Silver Stream (which we call the Milky Way), and examined the signs of the Zodiac,—the *Hwang-tao*, or Yellow Road,—and consulted the table of the Five *Hin*, or Principles of the Universe, and the mystical books of the alchemists. And after a long silence, he made answer to her, saying: "Gold and brass will never meet in wedlock, silver and iron never will embrace, until the flesh of a maiden be melted in the crucible; until the blood of a virgin be mixed with the metals in their fusion." So Ko-Ngai returned home sorrowful at heart; but she kept secret all that she had heard, and told no one what she had done.

At last came the awful day when the third and last effort to cast the great bell was to be made; and Ko-Ngai, together with her waiting-woman, accompanied her father to the foundry, and they took their places upon a platform overlooking the toiling of the moulders and the lava of liquefied metal. All the workmen wrought their tasks in silence; there was no sound heard but the muttering of the fires. And the muttering deepened into a roar like the roar of typhoons approaching, and the blood-red lake of metal slowly brightened like the vermilion of a sunrise, and the vermilion was transmuted into a radiant glow of gold, and the gold whitened blindingly, like the silver face of a full moon. Then the workers ceased to feed the raving flame, and all fixed their eyes upon the eyes of Kouan-Yu; and Kouan-Yu prepared to give the signal to cast.

But ere ever he lifted his finger, a cry caused him to turn his head; and all heard the voice of Ko-Ngai sounding sharply sweet as a bird's song above the great thunder of the fires,—*"For thy sake, O my Father!"* And even as she cried, she leaped into the white flood of metal; and the lava of the furnace roared to receive her, and spattered monstrous flakes of flame to the roof, and burst over the verge of the earthen crater, and cast up a whirling fountain of many-colored fires, and subsided quakingly, with lightnings and with thunders and with mutterings.

Then the father of Ko-Ngai, wild with his grief, would have leaped in after her, but that strong men held him back and kept firm grasp upon him until he had fainted away and they could bear him like one dead to his home. And the serving-woman of Ko-Ngai, dizzy and speechless for pain, stood before the furnace, still holding in her hands a shoe, a tiny, dainty shoe, with embroidery of pearls and flowers,—the shoe of her beautiful mistress that was. For she had sought to grasp Ko-Ngai by the foot as she leaped, but had only been able to clutch the shoe, and the pretty shoe came off in her hand; and she continued to stare at it like one gone mad.

But in spite of all these things, the command of the Celestial and August had to be obeyed, and the work of the moulders to be finished, hopeless as the result might be. Yet the glow of the metal seemed purer and whiter than before; and there was no sign of the beautiful body that had been entombed therein. So the ponderous casting was made; and lo! when the metal had become cool, it was found that the bell was beautiful to look upon, and perfect in form, and wonderful in color above all other bells. Nor was there any trace found of the body of Ko-Ngai; for it had been totally absorbed by the precious alloy, and blended with the well-blended brass and gold, with the intermingling of the silver and the iron. And when they sounded the bell, its tones were found to be deeper and mellower and mightier than the tones of any other bell,—

reaching even beyond the distance of one hundred *li*, like a pealing of summer thunder; and yet also like some vast voice uttering a name, a woman's name,— the name of Ko-Ngai!

And still, between each mighty stroke there is a long low moaning heard; and ever the moaning ends with a sound of sobbing and of complaining, as though a weeping woman should murmur, *"Hiai!"* And still, when the people hear that great golden moan they keep silence; but when the sharp, sweet shuddering comes in the air, and the sobbing of *"Hiai!"* then, indeed, do all the Chinese mothers in all the many-colored ways of Pe-king whisper to their little ones: *"Listen! that is Ko-Ngai crying for her shoe! That is Ko-Ngai calling for her shoe!"*

THE ANCIENT WORDS OF KOUEI—MASTER OF MUSICIANS IN THE COURTS OF THE EMPEROR YAO:—

When ye make to resound the stone melodious, the Ming-Khieou,—
When ye touch the lyre that is called Kin, or the guitar that is called Ssé,—
Accompanying their sound with song,—
Then do the grandfather and the father return;
Then do the ghosts of the ancestors come to hear.

The Story of Ming-Y

Sang the Poet Tching-Kou: "Surely the Peach-Flowers blossom over the tomb of Sië-Thao."

Do you ask me who she was,—the beautiful Sië-Thao? For a thousand years and more the trees have been whispering above her bed of stone. And the syllables of her name come to the listener with the lisping of the leaves; with the quivering of many-fingered boughs; with the fluttering of lights and shadows; with the breath, sweet as a woman's presence, of numberless savage flowers,—Sië-Thao. But, saving the whispering of her name, what the trees say cannot be understood; and they alone remember the years of

9

Sië-Thao. Something about her you might, neverthe-less, learn from any of those *Kiang-kou-jin,*—those famous Chinese story-tellers, who nightly narrate to listening crowds, in consideration of a few *tsien,* the legends of the past. Something concerning her you may also find in the book entitled "Kin-Kou-Ki-Koan," which signifies in our tongue: "The Marvellous Happenings of Ancient and of Recent Times." And perhaps of all things therein written, the most marvel-lous is this memory of Sië-Thao:—

Five hundred years ago, in the reign of the Emperor Houng-Wou, whose dynasty was *Ming,* there lived in the City of Genii, the city of Kwang-tchau-fu, a man celebrated for his learning and for his piety, named Tien-Pelou. This Tien-Pelou had one son, a beautiful boy, who for scholarship and for bodily grace and for polite accomplishments had no superior among the youths of his age. And his name was Ming-Y.

Now when the lad was in his eighteenth summer, it came to pass that Pelou, his father, was appointed Inspector of Public Instruction at the city of Tching-tou; and Ming-Y accompanied his parents thither. Near the city of Tching-tou lived a rich man of rank, a high commissioner of the government, whose name was Tchang, and who wanted to find a worthy teacher for his children. On hearing of the arrival of the new Inspector of Public Instruction, the noble Tchang vis-ited him to obtain advice in this matter; and happen-ing to meet and converse with Pelou's accomplished son, immediately engaged Ming-Y as a private tutor for his family.

Now as the house of this Lord Tchang was situated several miles from town, it was deemed best that Ming-Y should abide in the house of his employer. Accordingly the youth made ready all things necessary for his new sojourn; and his parents, bidding him farewell, counselled him wisely, and cited to him the words of Lao-tseu and of the ancient sages:

"By a beautiful face the world is filled with love; but Heaven may never be deceived thereby. Shouldst thou behold a woman coming from the East, look thou to the West; shouldst thou perceive a maiden approaching from the West, turn thine eyes to the East."

If Ming-Y did not heed this counsel in after days, it was only because of his youth and the thoughtlessness of a naturally joyous heart.

And he departed to abide in the house of Lord Tchang, while the autumn passed, and the winter also.

When the time of the second moon of spring was drawing near, and that happy day which the Chinese call *Hoa-tchao*, or, "The Birthday of a Hundred Flowers," a longing came upon Ming-Y to see his parents; and he opened his heart to the good Tchang, who not only gave him the permission he desired, but also pressed into his hand a silver gift of two ounces, thinking that the lad might wish to bring some little memento to his father and mother. For it is the Chinese custom, on the feast of Hoa-tchao, to make presents to friends and relations.

That day all the air was drowsy with blossom perfume, and vibrant with the droning of bees. It seemed

to Ming-Y that the path he followed had not been
trodden by any other for many long years; the grass
was tall upon it; vast trees on either side interlocked
their mighty and moss-grown arms above him, beshad-
owing the way; but the leafy obscurities quivered with
bird-song, and the deep vistas of the wood were glori-
fied by vapors of gold, and odorous with flower-
breathings as a temple with incense. The dreamy joy
of the day entered into the heart of Ming-Y; and he sat
him down among the young blossoms, under the
branches swaying against the violet sky, to drink in the
perfume and the light, and to enjoy the great sweet
silence. Even while thus reposing, a sound caused him
to turn his eyes toward a shady place where wild
peach-trees were in bloom; and he beheld a young
woman, beautiful as the pinkening blossoms themselves, trying to hide among them. Though he looked
for a moment only, Ming-Y could not avoid discerning
the loveliness of her face, the golden purity of her
complexion, and the brightness of her long eyes, that
sparkled under a pair of brows as daintily curved as
the wings of the silkworm butterfly outspread. Ming-Y
at once turned his gaze away, and, rising quickly, proceeded on his journey. But so much embarrassed did
he feel at the idea of those charming eyes peeping at
him through the leaves, that he suffered the money he
had been carrying in his sleeve to fall, without being
aware of it. A few moments later he heard the patter
of light feet running behind him, and a woman's voice
calling him by name. Turning his face in great surprise, he saw a comely servant-maid, who said to him,

"Sir, my mistress bade me pick up and return you this silver which you dropped upon the road." Ming-Y thanked the girl gracefully, and requested her to convey his compliments to her mistress. Then he proceeded on his way through the perfumed silence, athwart the shadows that dreamed along the forgotten path, dreaming himself also, and feeling his heart beating with strange quickness at the thought of the beautiful being that he had seen.

It was just such another day when Ming-Y, returning by the same path, paused once more at the spot where the gracious figure had momentarily appeared before him. But this time he was surprised to perceive, through a long vista of immense trees, a dwelling that had previously escaped his notice,—a country residence, not large, yet elegant to an unusual degree. The bright blue tiles of its curved and serrated double roof, rising above the foliage, seemed to blend their color with the luminous azure of the day; the green-and-gold designs of its carven porticos were exquisite artistic mockeries of leaves and flowers bathed in sunshine. And at the summit of terrace-steps before it, guarded by great porcelain tortoises, Ming-Y saw standing the mistress of the mansion,—the idol of his passionate fancy,—accompanied by the same waiting-maid who had borne to her his message of gratitude. While Ming-Y looked, he perceived that their eyes were upon him; they smiled and conversed together as if speaking about him; and, shy though he was, the youth found courage to salute the fair one from a distance. To his astonishment, the young servant beck-

oned him to approach; and opening a rustic gate half
veiled by trailing plants bearing crimson flowers,
Ming-Y advanced along the verdant alley leading to
the terrace, with mingled feelings of surprise and
timid joy. As he drew near, the beautiful lady with-
drew from sight; but the maid waited at the broad
steps to receive him, and said as he ascended:

"Sir, my mistress understands you wish to thank her
for the trifling service she recently bade me do you,
and requests that you will enter the house, as she
knows you already by repute, and desires to have the
pleasure of bidding you good-day."

Ming-Y entered bashfully, his feet making no sound
upon a matting elastically soft as forest moss, and
found himself in a reception-chamber vast, cool, and
fragrant with scent of blossoms freshly gathered. A
delicious quiet pervaded the mansion; shadows of flying birds passed over the bands of light that fell
through the half-blinds of bamboo; great butterflies,
with pinions of fiery color, found their way in, to hover
a moment about the painted vases, and pass out again
into the mysterious woods. And noiselessly as they, the
young mistress of the mansion entered by another
door, and kindly greeted the boy, who lifted his hands
to his breast and bowed low in salutation. She was
taller than he had deemed her, and supplely-slender
as a beauteous lily; her black hair was interwoven with
the creamy blossoms of the *chu-sha-kih;* her robes of
pale silk took shifting tints when she moved, as vapors
change hue with the changing of the light.

"If I be not mistaken," she said, when both had

seated themselves after having exchanged the customary formalities of politeness, "my honored visitor is none other than Tien-chou, surnamed Ming-Y, educator of the children of my respected relative, the High Commissioner Tchang. As the family of Lord Tchang is my family also, I cannot but consider the teacher of his children as one of my own kin."

"Lady," replied Ming-Y, not a little astonished, "may I dare to inquire the name of your honored family, and to ask the relation which you hold to my noble patron?"

"The name of my poor family," responded the comely lady, "is *Ping*,—an ancient family of the city of Tching-tou. I am the daughter of a certain Sië of Moun-hao; Sië is my name, likewise; and I was married to a young man of the Ping family, whose name was Khang. By this marriage I became related to your excellent patron; but my husband died soon after our wedding, and I have chosen this solitary place to reside in during the period of my widowhood."

There was a drowsy music in her voice, as of the melody of brooks, the murmurings of spring; and such a strange grace in the manner of her speech as Ming-Y had never heard before. Yet, on learning that she was a widow, the youth would not have presumed to remain long in her presence without a formal invitation; and after having sipped the cup of rich tea presented to him, he arose to depart. Sië would not suffer him to go so quickly.

"Nay, friend," she said; "stay yet a little while in my house, I pray you; for, should your honored patron

ever learn that you had been here, and that I had not
treated you as a respected guest, and regaled you even
as I would him, I know that he would be greatly
angered. Remain at least to supper."

So Ming-Y remained, rejoicing secretly in his heart,
for Sië seemed to him the fairest and sweetest being
he had ever known, and he felt that he loved her even
more than his father and his mother. And while they
talked the long shadows of the evening slowly blended
into one violet darkness; the great citron-light of the
sunset faded out; and those starry beings that are
called the Three Councillors, who preside over life
and death and the destinies of men, opened their cold
bright eyes in the northern sky. Within the mansion of
Sië the painted lanterns were lighted; the table was
laid for the evening repast; and Ming-Y took his place
at it, feeling little inclination to eat, and thinking only
of the charming face before him. Observing that he
scarcely tasted the dainties laid upon his plate, Sië
pressed her young guest to partake of wine; and they
drank several cups together. It was a purple wine, so
cool that the cup into which it was poured became
covered with vapory dew; yet it seemed to warm the
veins with strange fire. To Ming-Y, as he drank, all
things became more luminous as by enchantment; the
walls of the chamber appeared to recede, and the roof
to heighten; the lamps glowed like stars in their chains,
and the voice of Sië floated to the boy's ears like some
far melody heard through the spaces of a drowsy
night. His heart swelled; his tongue loosened; and
words flitted from his lips that he had fancied he could

never dare to utter. Yet Sië sought not to restrain him; her lips gave no smile; but her long bright eyes seemed to laugh with pleasure at his words of praise, and to return his gaze of passionate admiration with affectionate interest.

"I have heard," she said, "of your rare talent, and of your many elegant accomplishments. I know how to sing a little, although I cannot claim to possess any musical learning; and now that I have the honor of finding myself in the society of a musical professor, I will venture to lay modesty aside, and beg you to sing a few songs with me. I should deem it no small gratification if you would condescend to examine my musical compositions."

"The honor and the gratification, dear lady," replied Ming-Y, "will be mine; and I feel helpless to express the gratitude which the offer of so rare a favor deserves."

The serving-maid, obedient to the summons of a little silver gong, brought in the music and retired. Ming-Y took the manuscripts, and began to examine them with eager delight. The paper upon which they were written had a pale yellow tint, and was light as a fabric of gossamer; but the characters were antiquely beautiful, as though they had been traced by the brush of Heï-song Ché-Tchoo himself,—that divine Genius of Ink, who is no bigger than a fly; and the signatures attached to the compositions were the signatures of Youen-tchin, Kao-pien, and Thou-mou,—mighty poets and musicians of the dynasty of Thang! Ming-Y could not repress a scream of delight at the sight of treasures so inestimable and so unique; scarcely could he summon resolution enough to permit them to leave his hands even for a moment.

"O Lady!" he cried, "these are veritably priceless things, surpassing in worth the treasures of all kings. This indeed is the handwriting of those great masters who sang five hundred years before our birth. How marvellously it has been preserved! Is not this the wondrous ink of which it was written: *Po-nien-jou-chi, i-tien-jou-ki,*—'After centuries I remain firm as stone, and the letters that I make like lacquer'? And how divine the charm of this composition!—the song of Kao-pien, prince of poets, and Governor of Sze-tchouen five hundred years ago!"

"Kao-pien! darling Kao-pien!" murmured Sië, with a singular light in her eyes. "Kao-pien is also my favorite. Dear Ming-Y, let us chant his verses together, to the melody of old,—the music of those grand years when men were nobler and wiser than to-day."

And their voices rose through the perfumed night like the voices of the wonder-birds,—of the Fung-hoang,—blending together in liquid sweetness. Yet a moment, and Ming-Y, overcome by the witchery of his companion's voice, could only listen in speechless ecstasy, while the lights of the chamber swam dim before his sight, and tears of pleasure trickled down his cheeks.

So the ninth hour passed; and they continued to converse, and to drink the cool purple wine, and to sing the songs of the years of Thang, until far into the night. More than once Ming-Y thought of departing; but each time Sië would begin, in that silver-sweet voice of hers, so wondrous a story of the great poets of the past, and of the women whom they loved, that he became as one entranced; or she would sing for him a song so strange that all his senses seemed to die except that of hearing. And at last, as she paused to pledge him in a cup of wine, Ming-Y could not restrain himself from putting his arm about her round neck and drawing her dainty head closer to him, and kissing the lips that were so much ruddier and sweeter than the wine. Then their lips separated no more;—the night grew old, and they knew it not.

The birds awakened, the flowers opened their eyes to the rising sun, and Ming-Y found himself at last compelled to bid his lovely enchantress farewell. Sië, accompanying him to the terrace, kissed him fondly and said, "Dear boy, come hither as often as you are able,—as often as your heart whispers you to come. I know that you are not of those without faith and truth, who betray secrets; yet, being so young, you might also be sometimes thoughtless; and I pray you never to forget that only the stars have been the witnesses of our love. Speak of it to no living person, dearest; and take with you this little souvenir of our happy night."

And she presented him with an exquisite and curious little thing,—a paper-weight in likeness of a couchant lion, wrought from a jade-stone yellow as that created by a rainbow in honor of Kong-fu-tze. Tenderly the boy kissed the gift and the beautiful hand that gave it. "May the Spirits punish me," he vowed, "if ever I knowingly give you cause to reproach me, sweetheart!" And they separated with mutual vows.

That morning, on returning to the house of Lord Tchang, Ming-Y told the first falsehood which had ever passed his lips. He averred that his mother had requested him thenceforward to pass his nights at home, now that the weather had become so pleasant; for, though the way was somewhat long, he was strong and active, and needed both air and healthy exercise. Tchang believed all Ming-Y said, and offered no objection. Accordingly the lad found himself enabled to pass all his evenings at the house of the beautiful Sië. Each night they devoted to the same pleasures which had made their first acquaintance so charming: they sang and conversed by turns; they played at chess,—the learned game invented by Wu-Wang, which is an imitation of war; they composed pieces of eighty rhymes upon the flowers, the trees, the clouds, the streams, the birds, the bees. But in all accomplishments Sië far excelled her young sweetheart. Whenever they played at chess, it was always Ming-Y's general, Ming-Y's *tsiang*, who was surrounded and vanquished; when they composed verses, Sië's poems were ever superior to his in harmony of word-coloring, in elegance of form, in classic loftiness of thought. And the themes they selected were always the most difficult,—those of the poets of the Thang dynasty; the songs they sang were also the songs of five hundred years before,— the songs of Youen-tchin, of Thou-mou, of Kao-pien above all, high poet and ruler of the province of Sze-tchouen.

So the summer waxed and waned upon their love,

and the luminous autumn came, with its vapors of phantom gold, its shadows of magical purple.

Then it unexpectedly happened that the father of Ming-Y, meeting his son's employer at Tching-tou, was asked by him: "Why must your boy continue to travel every evening to the city, now that the winter is approaching? The way is long, and when he returns in the morning he looks fordone with weariness. Why not permit him to slumber in my house during the season of snow?" And the father of Ming-Y, greatly astonished, responded: "Sir, my son has not visited the city, nor has he been to our house all this summer. I fear that he must have acquired wicked habits, and that he passes his nights in evil company,—perhaps in gaming, or in drinking with the women of the flower-boats." But the High Commissioner returned: "Nay! that is not to be thought of. I have never found any evil in the boy, and there are no taverns nor flower-boats nor any places of dissipation in our neighborhood. No doubt Ming-Y has found some amiable youth of his own age with whom to spend his evenings, and only told me an untruth for fear that I would not otherwise permit him to leave my residence. I beg that you will say nothing to him until I shall have sought to discover this mystery; and this very evening I shall send my servant to follow after him, and to watch whither he goes."

Pelou readily assented to this proposal, and promising to visit Tchang the following morning, returned to his home. In the evening, when Ming-Y left the house of Tchang, a servant followed him unobserved at a distance. But on reaching the most obscure portion of the road, the boy disappeared from sight as suddenly as though the earth had swallowed him. After having long sought after him in vain, the domestic returned in great bewilderment to the house, and related what had taken place. Tchang immediately sent a messenger to Pelou.

In the mean time Ming-Y, entering the chamber of his beloved, was surprised and deeply pained to find her in tears. "Sweetheart," she sobbed, wreathing her arms around his neck, "we are about to be separated forever, because of reasons which I cannot tell you. From the very first I knew this must come to pass; and nevertheless it seemed to me for the moment so cruelly sudden a loss, so unexpected a misfortune, that I could not prevent myself from weeping! After this night we shall never see each other again, beloved, and I know that you will not be able to forget me while you live; but I know also that you will become a great scholar, and that honors and riches will be showered upon you, and that some beautiful and loving woman will console you for my loss. And now let us speak no more of grief; but let us pass this last evening joyously, so that your recollection of me may not be a painful one, and that you may remember my laughter rather than my tears."

She brushed the bright drops away, and brought wine and music and the melodious *kin* of seven silken strings, and would not suffer Ming-Y to speak for one moment of the coming separation. And she sang him an ancient song about the calmness of summer lakes reflecting the blue of heaven only, and the calmness of the heart also, before the clouds of care and of grief and of weariness darken its little world. Soon they forgot their sorrow in the joy of song and wine; and those last hours seemed to Ming-Y more celestial than even the hours of their first bliss.

But when the yellow beauty of morning came their sadness returned, and they wept. Once more Sië accompanied her lover to the terrace-steps; and as she kissed him farewell, she pressed into his hand a parting gift,—a little brush-case of agate, wonderfully chiselled, and worthy the table of a great poet. And they separated forever, shedding many tears.

Still Ming-Y could not believe it was an eternal parting. "No!" he thought, "I shall visit her tomorrow; for I cannot now live without her, and I feel assured that she cannot refuse to receive me." Such were the thoughts that filled his mind as he reached the house of Tchang, to find his father and his patron standing on the porch awaiting him. Ere he could speak a word, Pelou demanded: "Son, in what place have you been passing your nights?"

Seeing that his falsehood had been discovered, Ming-Y dared not make any reply, and remained abashed and silent, with bowed head, in the presence of his father. Then Pelou, striking the boy violently with his staff, commanded him to divulge the secret; and at last, partly through fear of his parent, and partly through fear of the law which ordains that *the son refusing to obey his father shall be punished with one hundred blows of the bamboo,*" Ming-Y faltered out the history of his love.

Tchang changed color at the boy's tale. "Child," exclaimed the High Commissioner, "I have no relative of the name of Ping; I have never heard of the woman you describe; I have never heard even of the house which you speak of. But I know also that you cannot dare to lie to Pelou, your honored father; there is some strange delusion in all this affair."

Then Ming-Y produced the gifts that Sië had given him,—the lion of yellow jade, the brush-case of carven agate, also some original compositions made by the beautiful lady herself. The astonishment of Tchang was now shared by Pelou. Both observed that the brush-case of agate and the lion of jade bore the appearance of objects that had lain buried in the earth for centuries, and were of a workmanship beyond the power of living man to imitate; while the compositions proved to be veritable master-pieces of poetry, written in the style of the poets of the dynasty of Thang.

"Friend Pelou," cried the High Commissioner, "let us immediately accompany the boy to the place where he obtained these miraculous things, and apply the testimony of our senses to this mystery. The boy is no doubt telling the truth; yet his story passes my understanding." And all three proceeded toward the place of the habitation of Sië.

But when they had arrived at the shadiest part of the road, where the perfumes were most sweet and the mosses were greenest, and the fruits of the wild peach flushed most pinkly, Ming-Y, gazing through the groves, uttered a cry of dismay. Where the azure-tiled roof had risen against the sky, there was now only the blue emptiness of air; where the green-and-gold façade had been, there was visible only the flickering of leaves under the aureate autumn light; and where the broad terrace had extended, could be discerned only a ruin,—a tomb so ancient, so deeply gnawed by moss, that the name graven upon it was no longer decipherable. The home of Sië had disappeared!

All suddenly the High Commissioner smote his forehead with his hand, and turning to Pelou, recited the well-known verse of the ancient poet Tching-Kou:—

"*Surely the peach-flowers blossom over the tomb of SIË-THAO.*"

"Friend Pelou," continued Tchang, "the beauty who bewitched your son was no other than she whose tomb stands there in ruin before us! Did she not say she was wedded to Ping-Khang? There is no family of that name, but Ping-Khang is indeed the name of a broad alley in the city near. There was a dark riddle in all that she said. She called herself Sië of Moun-Hiao: there is no person of that name; there is no street of that name; but the Chinese characters *Moun* and *hiao,* placed together, form the character 'Kiao.' Listen! The alley Ping-Khang, situated in the street Kiao, was the place where dwelt the great courtesans of the dynasty of Thang! Did she not sing the songs of Kao-pien? And upon the brush-case and the paper-weight she gave your son, are there not characters which read, '*Pure object of art belonging to Kao, of the city of Pho-hai*'? That city no longer exists; but the memory of Kao-pien remains, for he was governor of the province of Sze-tchouen, and a mighty poet. And when he dwelt in the land of Chou, was not his favorite the beautiful wanton Sië,—Sië-Thao, unmatched for grace among all the women of her day? It was he who made her a gift of those manuscripts of song; it was he who gave her those objects of rare art. Sië-Thao died not as other women die. Her limbs may have crumbled to dust; yet something of her still lives in this deep wood,—her Shadow still haunts this shadowy place."

Tchang ceased to speak. A vague fear fell upon the three. The thin mists of the morning made dim the distances of green, and deepened the ghostly beauty of the woods. A faint breeze passed by, leaving a trail of blossom-scent,—a last odor of dying flowers,—thin as that which clings to the silk of a forgotten robe; and, as it passed, the trees seemed to whisper across the silence, "*Sië-Thao.*"

Fearing greatly for his son, Pelou sent the lad away at once to the city of Kwang-tchau-fu. And there, in after years, Ming-Y obtained high dignities and honors by reason of his talents and his learning; and he married the daughter of an illustrious house, by whom he became the father of sons and daughters famous for their virtues and their accomplishments. Never could he forget Sië-Thao; and yet it is said that he never spoke of her,—not even when his children begged him to tell them the story of two beautiful objects that always lay upon his writing-table: a lion of yellow jade, and a brush-case of carven agate.

A SOUND OF GONGS, A SOUND OF SONG,—THE SONG
OF THE BUILDERS BUILDING THE DWELLINGS OF
THE DEAD:—

> *Khiû tchî yîng-yîng.*
> *Toû tchî hoûng-hoûng.*
> *Tchŏ tchî tông-tông.*
> *Siŏ liú pîng-pîng.*

The Legend of Tchi-Niu

In the quaint commentary accompanying the text of
that holy book of Lao-tseu called *Kan-ing-p'ien*
may be found a little story so old that the name of the
one who first told it has been forgotten for a thousand
years, yet so beautiful that it lives still in the memory
of four hundred millions of people, like a prayer that,
once learned, is forever remembered. The Chinese
writer makes no mention of any city nor of any province, although even in the relation of the most ancient
traditions such an omission is rare; we are only told
that the name of the hero of the legend was Tong-
yong, and that he lived in the years of the great dynasty of Han, some twenty centuries ago.

Tong-Yong's mother had died while he was yet an infant; and when he became a youth of nineteen years his father also passed away, leaving him utterly alone in the world, and without resources of any sort; for, being a very poor man, Tong's father had put himself to great straits to educate the lad, and had not been able to lay by even one copper coin of his earnings. And Tong lamented greatly to find himself so destitute that he could not honor the memory of that good father by having the customary rites of burial performed, and a carven tomb erected upon a propitious site. The poor only are friends of the poor; and among all those whom Tong knew; there was no one able to assist him in defraying the expenses of the funeral. In one way only could the youth obtain money,—by selling himself as a slave to some rich cultivator; and this he at last decided to do. In vain his friends did their utmost to dissuade him; and to no purpose did they attempt to delay the accomplishment of his sacrifice by beguiling promises of future aid. Tong only replied that he would sell his freedom a hundred times, if it were possible, rather than suffer his father's memory to remain unhonored even for a brief season. And furthermore, confiding in his youth and strength, he determined to put a high price upon his servitude,—a price which would enable him to build a handsome tomb, but which it would be well-nigh impossible for him ever to repay.

Accordingly he repaired to the broad public place where slaves and debtors were exposed for sale, and seated himself upon a bench of stone, having affixed

to his shoulders a placard inscribed with the terms of
his servitude and the list of his qualifications as a
laborer. Many who read the characters upon the placard smiled disdainfully at the price asked, and passed
on without a word; others lingered only to question
him out of simple curiosity; some commended him
with hollow praise; some openly mocked his unselfish-
ness, and laughed at his childish piety. Thus many
hours wearily passed, and Tong had almost despaired
of finding a master, when there rode up a high official
of the province,—a grave and handsome man, lord of
a thousand slaves, and owner of vast estates. Reining
in his Tartar horse, the official halted to read the placard and to consider the value of the slave. He did not
smile, or advise, or ask any questions; but having
observed the price asked, and the fine strong limbs of
the youth, purchased him without further ado, merely
ordering his attendant to pay the sum and to see that
the necessary papers were made out.

Thus Tong found himself enabled to fulfil the wish
of his heart, and to have a monument built which,
although of small size, was destined to delight the eyes
of all who beheld it, being designed by cunning artists
and executed by skilful sculptors. And while it was yet
designed only, the pious rites were performed, the
silver coin was placed in the mouth of the dead, the
white lanterns were hung at the door, the holy prayers
were recited, and paper shapes of all things the
departed might need in the land of the Genii were
consumed in consecrated fire. And after the geo-
mancers and the necromancers had chosen a burial

spot which no unlucky star could shine upon, a place of rest which no demon or dragon might ever disturb, the beautiful *chih* was built. Then was the phantom money strewn along the way; the funeral procession departed from the dwelling of the dead, and with prayers and lamentation the mortal remains of Tong's good father were borne to the tomb.

Then Tong entered as a slave into the service of his purchaser, who allotted him a little hut to dwell in; and thither Tong carried with him those wooden tablets, bearing the ancestral names, before which filial piety must daily burn the incense of prayer, and perform the tender duties of family worship.

Thrice had spring perfumed the breast of the land with flowers, and thrice had been celebrated that festival of the dead which is called *Siu-fan-ti,* and thrice had Tong swept and garnished his father's tomb and presented his fivefold offering of fruits and meats. The period of mourning had passed, yet he had not ceased to mourn for his parent. The years revolved with their moons, bringing him no hour of joy, no day of happy rest; yet he never lamented his servitude, or failed to perform the rites of ancestral worship,—until at last the fever of the rice-fields laid strong hold upon him, and he could not arise from his couch; and his fellow-laborers thought him destined to die. There was no one to wait upon him, no one to care for his needs, inasmuch as slaves and servants were wholly busied with the duties of the household or the labor of the fields,—all departing to toil at sunrise and returning weary only after the sundown.

Now, while the sick youth slumbered the fitful slumber of exhaustion one sultry noon, he dreamed that a strange and beautiful woman stood by him, and bent above him and touched his forehead with the long, fine fingers of her shapely hand. And at her cool touch a weird sweet shock passed through him, and all his veins tingled as if thrilled by new life. Opening his eyes in wonder, he saw verily bending over him the charming being of whom he had dreamed, and he knew that her lithe hand really caressed his throbbing forehead. But the flame of the fever was gone, a delicious coolness now penetrated every fibre of his body, and the thrill of which he had dreamed still tingled in his blood like a great joy. Even at the same moment the eyes of the gentle visitor met his own, and he saw they were singularly beautiful, and shone like splendid black jewels under brows curved like the wings of the swallow. Yet their calm gaze seemed to pass through him as light through crystal; and a vague awe came upon him, so that the question which had risen to his lips found no utterance. Then she, still caressing him, smiled and said: "I have come to restore thy strength and to be thy wife. Arise and worship with me."

Her clear voice had tones melodious as a bird's song; but in her gaze there was an imperious power which Tong felt he dare not resist. Rising from his couch, he was astounded to find his strength wholly restored; but the cool, slender hand which held his own led him away so swiftly that he had little time for amazement. He would have given years of existence for courage to speak of his misery, to declare his utter inability to maintain a wife; but something irresistible in the long dark eyes of his companion forbade him to speak; and as though his inmost thought had been discerned by that wondrous gaze, she said to him, in the same clear voice, "*I will provide.*" Then shame made him blush at the thought of his wretched aspect and tattered apparel; but he observed that she also was poorly attired, like a woman of the people,— wearing no ornament of any sort, nor even shoes upon her feet. And before he had yet spoken to her, they came before the ancestral tablets; and there she knelt with him and prayed, and pledged him in a cup of wine,—brought he knew not from whence,—and together they worshipped Heaven and Earth. Thus she became his wife.

A mysterious marriage it seemed, for neither on that day nor at any future time could Tong venture to ask his wife the name of her family, or of the place whence she came, and he could not answer any of the curious questions which his fellow-laborers put to him concerning her; and she, moreover, never uttered a word about herself, except to say that her name was Tchi. But although Tong had such awe of her that while her eyes were upon him he was as one having no will of his own, he loved her unspeakably; and the thought of his serfdom ceased to weigh upon him from the hour of his marriage. As through magic the little dwelling had become transformed: its misery was masked with charming paper devices,—with dainty decorations created out of nothing by that pretty jugglery of which woman only knows the secret.

Each morning at dawn the young husband found a well-prepared and ample repast awaiting him, and each evening also upon his return; but the wife all day sat at her loom, weaving silk after a fashion unlike anything which had ever been seen before in that province. For as she wove, the silk flowed from the loom like a slow current of glossy gold, bearing upon its undulations strange forms of violet and crimson and jewel-green: shapes of ghostly horsemen riding upon horses, and of phantom chariots dragon-drawn, and of standards of trailing cloud. In every dragon's beard glimmered the mystic pearl; in every rider's helmet sparkled the gem of rank. And each day Tchi would weave a great piece of such figured silk; and the fame of her weaving spread abroad. From far and near people thronged to see the marvellous work; and the silk-merchants of great cities heard of it, and they sent messengers to Tchi, asking her that she should weave for them and teach them her secret. Then she wove for them, as they desired, in return for the silver cubes which they brought her; but when they prayed her to teach them, she laughed and said, "Assuredly I could never teach you, for no one among you has fingers like mine." And indeed no man could discern her fingers when she wove, any more than he might behold the wings of a bee vibrating in swift flight.

The seasons passed, and Tong never knew want, so well did his beautiful wife fulfil her promise,—"*I will provide*"; and the cubes of bright silver brought by the silk-merchants were piled up higher and higher in the great carven chest which Tchi had bought for the storage of the household goods.

One morning, at last, when Tong, having finished his repast, was about to depart to the fields, Tchi unexpectedly bade him remain; and opening the great chest, she took out of it and gave him a document written in the official characters called *li-shu*. And Tong, looking at it, cried out and leaped in his joy, for it was the certificate of his manumission. Tchi had secretly purchased her husband's freedom with the price of her wondrous silks!

"Thou shalt labor no more for any master," she said, "but for thine own sake only. And I have also bought this dwelling, with all which is therein, and the tea-fields to the south, and the mulberry groves hard by,—all of which are thine."

Then Tong, beside himself for gratefulness, would have prostrated himself in worship before her, but that she would not suffer it.

Thus he was made free; and prosperity came to him with his freedom; and whatsoever he gave to the sacred earth was returned to him centupled; and his servants loved him and blessed the beautiful Tchi, so silent and yet so kindly to all about her. But the silk-loom soon remained untouched, for Tchi gave birth to a son,—a boy so beautiful that Tong wept with delight when he looked upon him. And thereafter the wife devoted herself wholly to the care of the child.

Now it soon became manifest that the boy was not less wonderful than his wonderful mother. In the third

month of his age he could speak; in the seventh month
he could repeat by heart the proverbs of the sages, and
recite the holy prayers; before the eleventh month he
could use the writing-brush with skill, and copy in
shapely characters the precepts of Lao-tseu. And the
priests of the temples came to behold him and to converse with him, and they marvelled at the charm of the
child and the wisdom of what he said; and they blessed
Tong, saying: "Surely this son of thine is a gift from the
Master of Heaven, a sign that the immortals love thee.
May thine eyes behold a hundred happy summers!"

It was in the Period of the Eleventh Moon: the
flowers had passed away, the perfume of the summer
had flown, the winds were growing chill, and in Tong's
home the evening fires were lighted. Long the husband and wife sat in the mellow glow,—he speaking
much of his hopes and joys, and of his son that was to
be so grand a man, and of many paternal projects;
while she, speaking little, listened to his words, and
often turned her wonderful eyes upon him with an
answering smile. Never had she seemed so beautiful
before; and Tong, watching her face, marked not how
the night waned, nor how the fire sank low, nor how
the wind sang in the leafless trees without.

All suddenly Tchi arose without speaking, and took
his hand in hers and led him, gently as on that strange
wedding-morning, to the cradle where their boy
slumbered, faintly smiling in his dreams. And in that
moment there came upon Tong the same strange fear
that he knew when Tchi's eyes had first met his
own,—the vague fear that love and trust had calmed,

but never wholly cast out, like unto the fear of the gods. And all unknowingly, like one yielding to the pressure of mighty invisible hands, he bowed himself low before her, kneeling as to a divinity. Now, when he lifted his eyes again to her face, he closed them forthwith in awe; for she towered before him taller than any mortal woman, and there was a glow about her as of sunbeams, and the light of her limbs shone through her garments. But her sweet voice came to him with all the tenderness of other hours, saying: *"Lo! my beloved, the moment has come in which I must forsake thee; for I was never of mortal born, and the Invisible may incarnate themselves for a time only. Yet I leave with thee the pledge of our love,— this fair son, who shall ever be to thee as faithful and as fond as thou thyself hast been. Know, my beloved, that I was sent to thee even by the Master of Heaven, in reward of thy filial piety, and that I must now return to the glory of His house: I AM THE GODDESS TCHI-NIU."*

Even as she ceased to speak, the great glow faded; and Tong, re-opening his eyes, knew that she had passed away forever,—mysteriously as pass the winds of heaven, irrevocably as the light of a flame blown out. Yet all the doors were barred, all the windows unopened. Still the child slept, smiling in his sleep. Outside, the darkness was breaking; the sky was brightening swiftly; the night was past. With splendid majesty the East threw open high gates of gold for the coming of the sun; and, illuminated by the glory of his coming, the vapors of morning wrought themselves into marvellous shapes of shifting color,—into forms weirdly beautiful as the silken dreams woven in the loom of Tchi-Niu.

篇應感上太

Before me ran, as a herald runneth, the Leader of the Moon;

And the Spirit of the Wind followed after me,— quickening his flight.

LI-SAO.

The Return of Yen-Tchin-King

In the thirty-eighth chapter of the holy book, *Kan-ing-p'ien*, wherein the Recompense of Immortality is considered, may be found the legend of Yen-Tchin-King. A thousand years have passed since the passing of the good Tchin-King; for it was in the period of the greatness of Thang that he lived and died.

Now, in those days when Yen-Tchin-King was Supreme Judge of one of the Six August Tribunals, one Li-hi-lié, a soldier mighty for evil, lifted the black banner of revolt, and drew after him, as a tide of destruction, the millions of the northern provinces. And learning of these things, and knowing also that Hi-lié was the most ferocious of men, who respected nothing on earth save fearlessness, the Son of Heaven commanded Tchin-King that he should visit Hi-lié and strive to recall the rebel to duty, and read unto the people who followed after him in revolt the Emperor's letter of reproof and warning. For Tchin-King was famed throughout the provinces for his wisdom, his rectitude, and his fearlessness; and the Son of Heaven believed that if Hi-lié would listen to the words of any living man steadfast in loyalty and virtue, he would listen to the words of Tchin-King. So Tchin-King arrayed himself in his robes of office, and set his house in order; and, having embraced his wife and his children, mounted his horse and rode away alone to the roaring camp of the rebels, bearing the Emperor's letter in his bosom. "I shall return; fear not!" were his last words to the gray servant who watched him from the terrace as he rode.

And Tchin-King at last descended from his horse, and entered into the rebel camp, and, passing through that huge gathering of war, stood in the presence of Hi-lié. High sat the rebel among his chiefs, encircled by the wave-lightning of swords and the thunders of ten thousand gongs: above him undulated the silken folds of the Black Dragon, while a vast fire rose bickering before him. Also Tchin-King saw that the tongues of that fire were licking human bones, and that skulls of men lay blackening among the ashes. Yet he was not afraid to look upon the fire, nor into the eyes of Hi-lié; but drawing from his bosom the roll of perfumed yellow silk upon which the words of the Emperor were written, and kissing it, he made ready to read, while the multitude became silent. Then, in a strong, clear voice he began:—

"The words of the Celestial and August, the Son of

Heaven, the Divine Ko-Tsu-Tchin-Yao-ti, unto the rebel Li-Hi-lié and those that follow him."

And a roar went up like the roar of the sea,—a roar of rage, and the hideous battle-moan, like the moan of a forest in storm,—*"Hoo! hoo-oo-oo-oo!"*—and the sword-lightnings brake loose, and the thunder of the gongs moved the ground beneath the messenger's feet. But Hi-lié waved his gilded wand, and again there was silence. "Nay!" spake the rebel chief; "let the dog bark!" So Tchin-King spake on:—

"Knowest thou not, O most rash and foolish of men, that thou leadest the people only into the mouth of the Dragon of Destruction? Knowest thou not, also, that the people of my kingdom are the first-born of the Master of Heaven? So it hath been written that he who doth needlessly subject the people to wounds and death shall not be suffered by Heaven to live! Thou who wouldst subvert those laws founded by the wise,—those laws in obedience to which may happiness and prosperity alone be found,—thou art committing the greatest of all crimes,—the crime that is never forgiven!

"O my people, think not that I your Emperor, I your Father, seek your destruction. I desire only your happiness, your prosperity, your greatness; let not your folly provoke the severity of your Celestial Parent. Follow not after madness and blind rage; hearken rather to the wise words of my messenger."

"Hoo! hoo-oo-oo-oo-oo!" roared the people, gathering fury. "Hoo! hoo-oo-oo-oo!"—till the mountains rolled back the cry like the rolling of a typhoon; and once more the pealing of the gongs paralyzed voice and hearing. Then Tchin-King, looking at Hi-lié, saw that he laughed, and that the words of the letter would not again be listened to. Therefore he read on to the end without looking about him, resolved to perform his mission in so far as lay in his power. And having read all, he would have given the letter to Hi-lié; but Hi-lié would not extend his hand to take it. Therefore Tchin-King replaced it in his bosom, and folding his arms, looked Hi-lié calmly in the face, and waited. Again Hi-lié waved his gilded wand; and the roaring ceased, and the booming of the gongs, until nothing save the fluttering of the Dragon-banner could be heard. Then spake Hi-lié, with an evil smile,—

"Tchin-King, O son of a dog! if thou dost not now take the oath of fealty, and bow thyself before me, and salute me with the salutation of Emperors,—even with the *luh-kao*, the triple prostration,—into that fire thou shalt be thrown."

But Tchin-King, turning his back upon the usurper, bowed himself a moment in worship to Heaven and Earth; and then rising suddenly, ere any man could lay hand upon him, he leaped into the towering flame, and stood there, with folded arms, like a God.

Then Hi-lié leaped to his feet in amazement, and shouted to his men; and they snatched Tchin-King from the fire, and wrung the flames from his robes with their naked hands, and extolled him, and praised him to his face. And even Hi-lié himself descended from his seat, and spoke fair words to him, saying: "O Tchin-King, I see thou art indeed a brave man and true, and worthy of all honor; be seated among us, I pray thee, and partake of whatever it is in our power to bestow!"

But Tchin-King, looking upon him unswervingly, replied in a voice clear as the voice of a great bell,—

"Never, O Hi-lié, shall I accept aught from thy hand, save death, so long as thou shalt continue in the path of wrath and folly. And never shall it be said that Tchin-King sat him down among rebels and traitors, among murderers and robbers."

Then Hi-lié in sudden fury, smote him with his sword; and Tchin-King fell to the earth and died, striving even in his death to bow his head toward the South,—toward the place of the Emperor's palace,—toward the presence of his beloved Master.

Even at the same hour the Son of Heaven, alone in the inner chamber of his palace, became aware of a Shape prostrate before his feet; and when he spake, the Shape arose and stood before him, and he saw that it was Tchin-King. And the Emperor would have questioned him; yet ere he could question, the familiar voice spake, saying:

"Son of Heaven, the mission confided to me I have performed; and thy command hath been accomplished to the extent of thy humble servant's feeble power. But even now must I depart, that I may enter the service of another Master."

And looking, the Emperor perceived that the Golden Tigers upon the wall were visible through the form of Tchin-King; and a strange coldness, like a winter wind, passed through the chamber; and the figure faded out. Then the Emperor knew that the Master of whom his faithful servant had spoken was none other than the Master of Heaven.

Also at the same hour the gray servant of Tchin-King's house beheld him passing through the apartments, smiling as he was wont to smile when he saw that all things were as he desired. "Is it well with thee, my lord?" questioned the aged man. And a voice answered him: "It is well"; but the presence of Tchin-King had passed away before the answer came.

So the armies of the Son of Heaven strove with the rebels. But the land was soaked with blood and blackened with fire; and the corpses of whole populations were carried by the rivers to feed the fishes of the sea; and still the war prevailed through many a long red year. Then came to aid the Son of Heaven the hordes that dwell in the desolations of the West and North,— horsemen born, a nation of wild archers, each mighty to bend a two-hundred-pound bow until the ears should meet. And as a whirlwind they came against rebellion, raining raven-feathered arrows in a storm of death; and they prevailed against Hi-lié and his people. Then those that survived destruction and defeat submitted, and promised allegiance; and once more was the law of righteousness restored. But Tchin-King had been dead for many summers.

And the Son of Heaven sent word to his victorious generals that they should bring back with them the bones of his faithful servant, to be laid with honor in a mausoleum erected by imperial decree. So the generals of the Celestial and August sought after the nameless grave and found it, and had the earth taken up, and made ready to remove the coffin.

But the coffin crumbled into dust before their eyes; for the worms had gnawed it, and the hungry earth had devoured its substance, leaving only a phantom shell that vanished at touch of the light. And lo! as it vanished, all beheld lying there the perfect form and features of the good Tchin-King. Corruption had not touched him, nor had the worms disturbed his rest, nor had the bloom of life departed from his face. And he seemed to dream only,—comely to see as upon the morning of his bridal, and smiling as the holy images smile, with eyelids closed, in the twilight of the great pagodas.

Then spoke a priest, standing by the grave: "O my children, this is indeed a Sign from the Master of Heaven; in such wise do the Powers Celestial preserve them that are chosen to be numbered with the Immortals. Death may not prevail over them, neither may corruption come nigh them. Verily the blessed Tchin-King hath taken his place among the divinities of Heaven!"

Then they bore Tchin-King back to his native place, and laid him with highest honors in the mausoleum which the Emperor had commanded; and there he sleeps, incorruptible forever, arrayed in his robes of state. Upon his tomb are sculptured the emblems of his greatness and his wisdom and his virtue, and the signs of his office, and the Four Precious Things: and the monsters which are holy symbols mount giant guard in stone about it; and the weird Dogs of Fo keep watch before it, as before the temples of the gods.

冀 可 僵 示 神

SANG A CHINESE HEART FOURTEEN HUNDRED YEARS
AGO:—

There is Somebody of whom I am thinking.
Far away there is Somebody of whom I am
thinking.
A hundred leagues of mountains lie between us:—
Yet the same Moon shines upon us, and the passing
Wind breathes upon us both.

The Tradition of the Tea-Plant

> "Good is the continence of the eye;
> Good is the continence of the ear;
> Good is the continence of the nostrils;
> Good is the continence of the tongue;
> Good is the continence of the body;
> Good is the continence of speech;
> Good is all. . . ."

Again the Vulture of Temptation soared to the
highest heaven of his contemplation, bringing his
soul down, down, reeling and fluttering, back to the
World of Illusion. Again the memory made dizzy his

47

thought, like the perfume of some venomous flower.
Yet he had seen the bayadere for an instant only, when
passing through Kasí upon his way to China,—to the
vast empire of souls that thirsted after the refreshment
of Buddha's law, as sun-parched fields thirst for the
life-giving rain. When she called him, and dropped
her little gift into his mendicant's bowl, he had indeed
lifted his fan before his face, yet not quickly enough;
and the penalty of that fault had followed him a thousand leagues,—pursued after him even into the strange
land to which he had come to bear the words of the
Universal Teacher. Accursed beauty! surely framed by
the Tempter of tempters, by Mara himself, for the
perdition of the just! Wisely had Bhagavat warned his
disciples: "O ye Çramanas, women are not to be
looked upon! And if ye chance to meet women, ye
must not suffer your eyes to dwell upon them; but,
maintaining holy reserve, speak not to them at all.
Then fail not to whisper unto your own hearts, 'Lo, we
are Çramanas, whose duty it is to remain uncontami-
nated by the corruptions of this world, even as the
Lotos, which suffereth no vileness to cling unto its
leaves, though it blossom amid the refuse of the way-
side ditch.'" Then also came to his memory, but with
a new and terrible meaning, the words of the Twentieth-
and-Third of the Admonitions:—

"Of all attachments unto objects of desire, the
strongest indeed is the attachment to form. Happily,
this passion is unique; for were there any other
like unto it, then to enter the Perfect Way were
impossible."

How, indeed, thus haunted by the illusion of form, was he to fulfil the vow that he had made to pass a night and a day in perfect and unbroken meditation? Already the night was beginning! Assuredly, for sickness of the soul, for fever of the spirit, there was no physic save prayer. The sunset was swiftly fading out. He strove to pray:—

"*O the Jewel in the Lotos!*

"Even as the tortoise withdraweth its extremities into its shell, let me, O Blessed One, withdraw my senses wholly into meditation!

"*O the Jewel in the Lotos!*

"For even as rain penetrateth the broken roof of a dwelling long uninhabited, so may passion enter the soul uninhabited by meditation.

"*O the Jewel in the Lotos!*

"Even as still water that hath deposited all its slime, so let my soul, O Tathâgata, be made pure! Give me strong power to rise above the world, O Master, even as the wild bird rises from its marsh to follow the pathway of the Sun!

"*O the Jewel in the Lotos!*

"By day shineth the sun, by night shineth the moon; shineth also the warrior in harness of war; shineth likewise in meditations the Çramana. But the Buddha at all times, by night or by day, shineth ever the same, illuminating the world.

"*O the Jewel in the Lotos!*

"Let me cease, O thou Perfectly Awakened, to remain as an Ape in the World-forest, forever ascending and descending in search of the fruits of folly.

Swift as the twining of serpents, vast as the growth of lianas in a forest, are the all-encircling growths of the Plant of Desire.

"O the Jewel in the Lotos!"

Vain his prayer, alas! vain also his invocation! The mystic meaning of the holy text—the sense of the Lotos, the sense of the Jewel—had evaporated from the words, and their monotonous utterance now served only to lend more dangerous definition to the memory that tempted and tortured him. *O the jewel in her ear!* What lotos-bud more dainty than the folded flower of flesh, with its dripping of diamond-fire! Again he saw it, and the curve of the cheek beyond, luscious to look upon as beautiful brown fruit. How true the Two Hundred and Eighty-Fourth verse of the Admonitions!—"So long as a man shall not have torn from his heart even the smallest rootlet of that liana of desire which draweth his thought toward women, even so long shall his soul remain fettered." And there came to his mind also the Three Hundred and Forty-Fifth verse of the same blessed book, regarding fetters:

"In bonds of rope, wise teachers have said, there is no strength; nor in fetters of wood, nor yet in fetters of iron. Much stronger than any of these is the fetter of *concern for the jewelled earrings of women.*"

"Omniscient Gotama!" he cried,—"all-seeing Tathâgata! How multiform the consolation of Thy Word! how marvellous Thy understanding of the human heart! Was this also one of Thy temptations?— one of the myriad illusions marshalled before Thee by

Mara in that night when the earth rocked as a chariot,
and the sacred trembling passed from sun to sun, from
system to system, from universe to universe, from
eternity to eternity?"

O the jewel in her ear! The vision would not go!
Nay, each time it hovered before his thought it seemed
to take a warmer life, a fonder look, a fairer form; to
develop with his weakness; to gain force from his
enervation. He saw the eyes, large, limpid, soft, and
black as a deer's; the pearls in the dark hair, and the
pearls in the pink mouth; the lips curling to a kiss, a
flower-kiss; and a fragrance seemed to float to his
senses, sweet, strange, soporific,—a perfume of youth,
an odor of woman. Rising to his feet, with strong
resolve he pronounced again the sacred invocation;
and he recited the holy words of the *Chapter of
Impermanency*:

"Gazing upon the heavens and upon the earth
ye must say, *These are not permanent*. Gazing upon
the mountains and the rivers, ye must say, *These are
not permanent*. Gazing upon the forms and upon the
faces of exterior beings, and beholding their growth
and their development, ye must say, *These are not
permanent*."

And nevertheless! how sweet illusion! The illusion
of the great sun; the illusion of the shadow-casting
hills; the illusion of waters, formless and multiform;
the illusion of—Nay, nay! what impious fancy! Accursed
girl! yet, yet! why should he curse her? Had she ever
done aught to merit the malediction of an ascetic?
Never, never! Only her form, the memory of her, the

beautiful phantom of her, the accursed phantom of her! What was she? An illusion creating illusions, a mockery, a dream, a shadow, a vanity, a vexation of spirit! The fault, the sin, was in himself, in his rebellious thought, in his untamed memory. Though mobile as water, intangible as vapor, Thought, nevertheless, may be tamed by the Will, may be harnessed to the chariot of Wisdom—must be!—that happiness be found. And he recited the blessed verses of the "Book of the Way of the Law":—

"*All forms are only temporary.*" When this great truth is fully comprehended by any one, then is he delivered from all pain. This is the Way of Purification.

"*All forms are subject unto pain.*" When this great truth is fully comprehended by any one, then is he delivered from all pain. This is the Way of Purification.

"*All forms are without substantial reality.*" When this great truth is fully comprehended by any one, then is he delivered from all pain. This is the way of . . .

Her form, too, unsubstantial, unreal, an illusion only, though comeliest of illusions? She had given him alms! Was the merit of the giver illusive also,—illusive like the grace of the supple fingers that gave? Assuredly there were mysteries in the Abhidharma impenetrable, incomprehensible! . . . It was a golden coin, stamped with the symbol of an elephant,—not more of an illusion, indeed, than the gifts of Kings to the Buddha! Gold upon her bosom also, less fine than the gold of her skin. Naked between the silken sash and the narrow breast-corslet, her young waist curved glossy and pliant as a bow. Richer the silver in her voice than in the hollow *pagals* that made a moonlight about her ankles! But her smile!—the little teeth like flower-stamens in the perfumed blossom of her mouth!

O weakness! O shame! How had the strong Charioteer of Resolve thus lost his control over the wild team of fancy! Was this languor of the Will a signal of coming peril, the peril of slumber? So strangely vivid those fancies were, so brightly definite, as about to take visible form, to move with factitious life, to play some unholy drama upon the stage of dreams! "O Thou Fully Awakened!" he cried aloud, "help now thy humble disciple to obtain the blessed wakefulness of perfect contemplation! let him find force to fulfil his vow! suffer not Mara to prevail against him!" And he recited the eternal verses of the Chapter of Wakefulness:—

"Completely and eternally awake are the disciples of Gotama! Unceasingly, by day and night, their thoughts are fixed upon the Law.

"Completely and eternally awake are the disciples of Gotama! Unceasingly, by day and night, their thoughts are fixed upon the Community.

"Completely and eternally awake are the disciples of Gotama! Unceasingly, by day and night, their thoughts are fixed upon the Body.

"Completely and eternally awake are the disciples of Gotama! Unceasingly, by day and night, their minds know the sweetness of perfect peace.

"Completely and eternally awake are the disciples of Gotama! Unceasingly, by day and night, their minds enjoy the deep peace of meditation."

There came a murmur to his ears; a murmuring of many voices, smothering the utterances of his own, like a tumult of waters. The stars went out before his sight; the heavens darkened their infinities: all things became viewless, became blackness; and the great murmur deepened, like the murmur of a rising tide; and the earth seemed to sink from beneath him. His feet no longer touched the ground; a sense of supernatural buoyancy pervaded every fibre of his body: he felt himself floating in obscurity; then sinking softly, slowly, like a feather dropped from the pinnacle of a temple. Was this death? Nay, for all suddenly, as transported by the Sixth Supernatural Power, he stood again in light,—a perfumed, sleepy light, vapory, beautiful,—that bathed the marvellous streets of some Indian city. Now the nature of the murmur became manifest to him; for he moved with a mighty throng, a people of pilgrims, a nation of worshippers. But these were not of his faith; they bore upon their foreheads the smeared symbols of obscene gods! Still, he could not escape from their midst; the mile-broad human torrent bore him irresistibly with it, as a leaf is swept by the waters of the Ganges. Rajahs were there with their trains, and princes riding upon elephants, and Brahmins robed in their vestments, and swarms of voluptuous dancing-girls, moving to chant of *kabit* and *damâri*. But whither, whither? Out of the city into the sun they passed, between avenues of banyan, down colonnades of palm. But whither, whither?

Blue-distant, a mountain of carven stone appeared before them,—the Temple, lifting to heaven its wilderness of chiselled pinnacles, flinging to the sky the golden spray of its decoration. Higher it grew with approach, the blue tones changed to gray, the outlines sharpened in the light. Then each detail became visible: the elephants of the pedestals standing upon tortoises of rock; the great grim faces of the capitals; the serpents and monsters writhing among the friezes; the many-headed gods of basalt in their galleries of fretted niches, tier above tier; the pictured foulnesses, the painted lusts, the divinities of abomination. And, yawning in the sloping precipice of sculpture, beneath a frenzied swarming of gods and Gopia,—a beetling pyramid of limbs and bodies interlocked,—the Gate, cavernous and shadowy as the mouth of Siva, devoured the living multitude.

The eddy of the throng whirled him with it to the vastness of the interior. None seemed to note his yellow robe, none even to observe his presence. Giant aisles intercrossed their heights above him; myriads of mighty pillars, fantastically carven, filed away to invisibility behind the yellow illumination of torch-fires. Strange images, weirdly sensuous, loomed up through haze of incense. Colossal figures, that at a distance assumed the form of elephants or garuda-birds, changed aspect when approached, and revealed as the secret of their design an interplaiting of the bodies of women; while one divinity rode all the monstrous

allegories,—one divinity or demon, eternally the same
in the repetition of the sculptor, universally visible as
though self-multiplied. The huge pillars themselves
were symbols, figures, carnalities; the orgiastic spirit
of that worship lived and writhed in the contorted
bronze of the lamps, the twisted gold of the cups, the
chiselled marble of the tanks. . . .

How far had he proceeded? He knew not; the journey among those countless columns, past those armies
of petrified gods, down lanes of flickering lights,
seemed longer than the voyage of a caravan, longer
than his pilgrimage to China! But suddenly, inexplica-
bly, there came a silence as of cemeteries; the living
ocean seemed to have ebbed away from about him, to
have been engulfed within abysses of subterranean
architecture! He found himself alone in some strange
crypt before a basin, shell-shaped and shallow, bearing
in its centre a rounded column of less than human
height, whose smooth and spherical summit was
wreathed with flowers. Lamps similarly formed, and
fed with oil of palm, hung above it. There was no other
graven image, no visible divinity. Flowers of countless
varieties lay heaped upon the pavement; they covered
its surface like a carpet, thick, soft; they exhaled their
ghosts beneath his feet. The perfume seemed to pen-
etrate his brain,—a perfume sensuous, intoxicating,
unholy; an unconquerable languor mastered his will,
and he sank to rest upon the floral offerings.

The sound of a tread, light as a whisper, approached
through the heavy stillness, with a drowsy tinkling of
pagals, a tintinnabulation of anklets. All suddenly he

felt glide about his neck the tepid smoothness of a woman's arm. *She, she!* his Illusion, his Temptation; but how transformed, transfigured!—preternatural in her loveliness, incomprehensible in her charm! Delicate as a jasmine-petal the cheek that touched his own; deep as night, sweet as summer, the eyes that watched him. *"Heart's-thief,"* her flower-lips whispered,— *"heart's-thief, how have I sought for thee! How have I found thee! Sweets I bring thee, my beloved; lips and bosom; fruit and blossom. Hast thirst? Drink from the well of mine eyes! Wouldst sacrifice? I am thine altar! Wouldst pray? I am thy God!"*

Their lips touched; her kiss seemed to change the cells of his blood to flame. For a moment Illusion triumphed; Mara prevailed! . . . With a shock of resolve the dreamer awoke in the night,—under the stars of the Chinese sky.

Only a mockery of sleep! But the vow had been violated, the sacred purpose unfulfilled! Humiliated, penitent, but resolved, the ascetic drew from his girdle a keen knife, and with unfaltering hands severed his eyelids from his eyes, and flung them from him. "O Thou Perfectly Awakened!" he prayed, "thy disciple hath not been overcome save through the feebleness of the body; and his vow hath been renewed. Here shall he linger, without food or drink, until the moment of its fulfilment." And having assumed the hieratic posture,—seated himself with his lower limbs folded beneath him, and the palms of his hands upward, the right upon the left, the left resting upon the sole of his upturned foot,—he resumed his meditation.

Dawn blushed; day brightened. The sun shortened all the shadows of the land, and lengthened them again, and sank at last upon his funeral pyre of crimson-burning cloud. Night came and glittered and passed. But Mara had tempted in vain. This time the vow had been fulfilled, the holy purpose accomplished.

And again the sun arose to fill the world with laughter of light; flowers opened their hearts to him; birds sang their morning hymn of fire worship; the deep forest trembled with delight; and far upon the plain, the eaves of many-storied temples and the peaked caps of the city-towers caught aureate glory. Strong in the holiness of his accomplished vow, the Indian pilgrim arose in the morning glow. He started for amazement as he lifted his hands to his eyes. What! was everything a dream? Impossible! Yet now his eyes felt no pain; neither were they lidless; not even so much as one of their lashes was lacking. What marvel had been wrought? In vain he looked for the severed lids that he had flung upon the ground; they had mysteriously vanished. But lo! there where he had cast them two wondrous shrubs were growing, with dainty leaflets eyelid-shaped, and snowy buds just opening to the East.

Then, by virtue of the supernatural power acquired in that mighty meditation, it was given the holy missionary to know the secret of that newly created plant,—the subtle virtue of its leaves. And he named it, in the language of the nation to whom he brought the Lotos of the Good Law, "*TE*"; and he spake to it, saying:—

"Blessed be thou, sweet plant, beneficent, life-giving, formed by the spirit of virtuous resolve! Lo! the fame of thee shall yet spread unto the ends of the earth; and the perfume of thy life be borne unto the uttermost parts by all the winds of heaven! Verily, for all time to come men who drink of thy sap shall find such refreshment that weariness may not overcome them nor languor seize upon them;—neither shall they know the confusion of drowsiness, nor any desire for slumber in the hour of duty or of prayer. Blessed be thou!"

And still, as a mist of incense, as a smoke of universal sacrifice, perpetually ascends to heaven from all the lands of earth the pleasant vapor of TE, created for the refreshment of mankind by the power of a holy vow, the virtue of a pious atonement.

It is written in the FONG-HO-CHIN-TCH'OUEN, *that whenever the artist Thsang-Kong was in doubt, he would look into the fire of the great oven in which his vases were baking, and question the Guardian-Spirit dwelling in the flame. And the Spirit of the Oven-fires so aided him with his counsels, that the porcelains made by Thsang-Kong were indeed finer and lovelier to look upon than all other porcelains. And they were baked in the years of Khang-hí,—sacredly called Jin Houang-tí.*

The Tale of the Porcelain-God

Who first of men discovered the secret of the *Kao-ling*, of the *Pe-tun-tse*,—the bones and the flesh, the skeleton and the skin, of the beauteous Vase? Who first discovered the virtue of the curd-white clay? Who first prepared the ice-pure bricks of *tun:* the gathered-hoariness of mountains that have died for age; blanched dust of the rocky bones and the stony flesh of sun-seeking Giants that have ceased to be? Unto whom was it first given to discover the divine art of porcelain?

61

Unto Pu, once a man, now a god, before whose snowy statues bow the myriad populations enrolled in the guilds of the potteries. But the place of his birth we know not; perhaps the tradition of it may have been effaced from remembrance by that awful war which in our own day consumed the lives of twenty millions of the Black-haired Race, and obliterated from the face of the world even the wonderful City of Porcelain itself,—the City of King-te-chin, that of old shone like a jewel of fire in the blue mountain-girdle of Feou-liang.

Before his time indeed the Spirit of the Furnace had being; had issued from the Infinite Vitality; had become manifest as an emanation of the Supreme Tao. For Hoang-ti, nearly five thousand years ago, taught men to make good vessels of baked clay; and in his time all potters had learned to know the God of Oven-fires, and turned their wheels to the murmuring of prayer. But Hoang-ti had been gathered unto his fathers for thrice ten hundred years before that man was born destined by the Master of Heaven to become the Porcelain-God.

And his divine ghost, ever hovering above the smoking and the toiling of the potteries, still gives power to the thought of the shaper, grace to the genius of the designer, luminosity to the touch of the enamellist. For by his heaven-taught wisdom was the art of porcelain created; by his inspiration were accomplished all the miracles of Thao-yu, maker of the *Kia-yu-ki*, and all the marvels made by those who followed after him;—

All the azure porcelains called *You-kouo-thien-tsing;* brilliant as a mirror, thin as paper of rice, sonorous as the melodious stone *Khing,* and colored, in obedience to the mandate of the Emperor Chi-tsong, "blue as the sky is after rain, when viewed through the rifts of the clouds." These were, indeed, the first of all porcelains, likewise called *Tchai-yao,* which no man, howsoever wicked, could find courage to break, for they charmed the eye like jewels of price;—

And the *Jou-yao,* second in rank among all porcelains, sometimes mocking the aspect and the sonority of bronze, sometimes blue as summer waters, and deluding the sight with mucid appearance of thickly floating spawn of fish;—

And the *Kouan-yao,* which are the Porcelains of Magistrates, and third in rank of merit among all wondrous porcelains, colored with colors of the morning,— skyey blueness, with the rose of a great dawn blushing and bursting through it, and long-limbed marsh-birds flying against the glow;

Also the *Ko-yao,*—fourth in rank among perfect porcelains,—of fair, faint, changing colors, like the body of a living fish, or made in the likeness of opal substance, milk mixed with fire; the work of Sing-I, elder of the immortal brothers Tchang;

Also the *Ting-yao,*—fifth in rank among all perfect porcelains,—white as the mourning garments of a spouse bereaved, and beautiful with a trickling as of tears,—the porcelains sung of by the poet Son-tong-po;

Also the porcelains called *Pi-se-yao,* whose colors are called "hidden," being alternately invisible and vis-

ible, like the tints of ice beneath the sun,—the porcelains celebrated by the far-famed singer Sin-in;

Also the wondrous *Chu-yao*,—the pallid porcelains
that utter a mournful cry when smitten,—the porcelains chanted of by the mighty chanter, Thou-
chao-ling;

Also the porcelains called *Thsin-yao*, white or blue,
surface-wrinkled as the face of water by the fluttering
of many fins. . . . And ye can see the fish!

Also the vases called *Tsi-hong-khi*, red as sunset
after a rain; and the *T'o-t'ai-khi*, fragile as the wings of
the silkworm-moth, lighter than the shell of an egg;

Also the *Kia-tsing*,—fair cups pearl-white when
empty, yet, by some incomprehensible witchcraft of
construction, seeming to swarm with purple fish the
moment they are filled with water;

Also the porcelains called *Yao-pien*, whose tints are
transmuted by the alchemy of fire; for they enter
blood-crimson into the heat, and change there to liz-
ard-green, and at last come forth azure as the cheek of
the sky;

Also the *Ki-tcheou-yao*, which are all violet as a
summer's night; and the *Hing-yao* that sparkle with
the sparklings of mingled silver and snow;

Also the *Sieouen-yao*,—some ruddy as iron in the
furnace, some diaphanous and ruby-red, some granu-
lated and yellow as the rind of an orange, some softly
flushed as the skin of a peach;

Also the *Tsoui-khi-yao*, crackled and green as
ancient ice is; and the *Tchou-fou-yao*, which are the
Porcelains of Emperors, with dragons wriggling and

snarling in gold; and those *yao* that are pink-ribbed
and have their angles serrated as the claws of crabs
are;

Also the *Ou-ni-yao,* black as the pupil of the eye,
and as lustrous; and the *Hou-tien-yao,* darkly yellow as
the faces of men of India; and the *Ou-kong-yao,* whose
color is the dead-gold of autumn-leaves;

Also the *Long-kang-yao,* green as the seedling of a
pea, but bearing also paintings of sun-silvered cloud,
and of the Dragons of Heaven;

Also the *Tching-hoa-yao,*—pictured with the amber
bloom of grapes and the verdure of vine-leaves and
the blossoming of poppies, or decorated in relief with
figures of fighting crickets;

Also the *Khang-hi-nien-ts'ang-yao,* celestial azure
sown with star-dust of gold; and the *Khien-long-nien-
thang-yao,* splendid in sable and silver as a fervid
night that is flashed with lightnings.

Not indeed the *Long-Ouang-yao,*—painted with
the lascivious *Pi-hi,* with the obscene *Nan-niu-ssé-sie,*
with the shameful *Tchun-hoa,* or "Pictures of Spring";
abominations created by command of the wicked
Emperor Moutsong, though the Spirit of the Furnace
hid his face and fled away;

But all other vases of startling form and substance,
magically articulated, and ornamented with figures in
relief, in cameo, in transparency,—the vases with ori-
fices belled like the cups of flowers, or cleft like the
bills of birds, or fanged like the jaws of serpents, or
pink-lipped as the mouth of a girl; the vases flesh-
colored and purple-veined and dimpled, with ears

and with earrings; the vases in likeness of mushrooms, of lotos-flowers, of lizards, of horse-footed dragons woman-faced; the vases strangely translucid, that simulate the white glimmering of grains of prepared rice, that counterfeit the vapory lace-work of frost, that imitate the efflorescences of coral;—

Also the statues in porcelain of divinities: the Genius of the Hearth; the Long-pinn who are the Twelve Deities of Ink; the blessed Lao-tseu, born with silver hair; Kong-fu-tse, grasping the scroll of written wisdom; Kouan-in, sweetest Goddess of Mercy, standing snowy-footed upon the heart of her golden lily; Chinong, the god who taught men how to cook; Fo, with long eyes closed in meditation, and lips smiling the mysterious smile of Supreme Beatitude; Cheou-lao, god of Longevity, bestriding his aërial steed, the white-winged stork; Pou-t'ai, Lord of Contentment and of Wealth, obese and dreamy; and that fairest Goddess of Talent, from whose beneficent hands eternally streams the iridescent rain of pearls.

And though many a secret of that matchless art that Pu bequeathed unto men may indeed have been forgotten and lost forever, the story of the Porcelain-God is remembered; and I doubt not that any of the aged *Jeou-yen-liao-kong*, any one of the old blind men of the great potteries, who sit all day grinding colors in the sun, could tell you Pu was once a humble Chinese workman, who grew to be a great artist by dint of tireless study and patience and by the inspiration of Heaven. So famed he became that some deemed him an alchemist, who possessed the secret called *White-*

and-Yellow, by which stones might be turned into gold; and others thought him a magician, having the ghastly power of murdering men with horror of nightmare, by hiding charmed effigies of them under the tiles of their own roofs; and others, again, averred that he was an astrologer who had discovered the mystery of those Five Hing which influence all things,—those Powers that move even in the currents of the star-drift, in the milky *Tien-ho,* or River of the Sky. Thus, at least, the ignorant spoke of him; but even those who stood about the Son of Heaven, those whose hearts had been strengthened by the acquisition of wisdom, wildly praised the marvels of his handicraft, and asked each other if there might be any imaginable form of beauty which Pu could not evoke from that beauteous substance so docile to the touch of his cunning hand.

And one day it came to pass that Pu sent a priceless gift to the Celestial and August: a vase imitating the substance of ore-rock, all aflame with pyritic scintillation,—a shape of glittering splendor with chameleons sprawling over it; chameleons of porcelain that shifted color as often as the beholder changed his position. And the Emperor, wondering exceedingly at the splendor of the work, questioned the princes and the mandarins concerning him that made it. And the princes and the mandarins answered that he was a workman named Pu, and that he was without equal among potters, knowing secrets that seemed to have been inspired either by gods or by demons. Whereupon the Son of Heaven sent his officers to Pu with a noble gift, and summoned him unto his presence.

So the humble artisan entered before the Emperor, and having performed the supreme prostration,—thrice kneeling, and thrice nine times touching the ground with his forehead,—awaited the command of the August.

And the Emperor spake to him, saying: "Son, thy gracious gift hath found high favor in our sight; and for the charm of that offering we have bestowed upon thee a reward of five thousand silver *liang*. But thrice that sum shall be awarded thee so soon as thou shalt have fulfilled our behest. Hearken, therefore, O matchless artificer! it is now our will that thou make for us a vase having the tint and the aspect of living flesh, but—mark well our desire!—*of flesh made to creep by the utterance of such words as poets utter,—flesh moved by an Idea, flesh horripilated by a Thought!* Obey, and answer not! We have spoken."

Now Pu was the most cunning of all the *P'ei-se-kong*,—the men who marry colors together; of all the *Hoa-yang-kong*, who draw the shapes of vase decoration; of all the *Hoei-sse-kong*, who paint in enamel; of all the *T'ien-thsai-kong*, who brighten color; of all the *Chao-lou-kong*, who watch the furnace-fires and the porcelain-ovens. But he went away sorrowing from the Palace of the Son of Heaven, notwithstanding the gift of five thousand silver *liang* which had been given to him. For he thought to himself: "Surely the mystery of the comeliness of flesh, and the mystery of that by which it is moved, are the secrets of the Supreme Tao. How shall man lend the aspect of sentient life to dead clay? Who save the Infinite can give soul?"

Now Pu had discovered those witchcrafts of color, those surprises of grace, that make the art of the ceramist. He had found the secret of the *feng-hong*, the wizard flush of the Rose; of the *hoa-hong*, the delicious incarnadine; of the mountain-green called *chan-lou;* of the pale soft yellow termed *hiao-hoang-yeou;* and of the *hoang-kin*, which is the blazing beauty of gold. He had found those eel-tints, those serpent-greens, those pansy-violets, those furnace-crimsons, those carmi-nates and lilacs, subtle as spirit-flame, which our enamellists of the Occident long sought without success to reproduce. But he trembled at the task assigned him, as he returned to the toil of his studio, saying: "How shall any miserable man render in clay the quivering of flesh to an Idea,—the inexplicable horripila-tion of a Thought? Shall a man venture to mock the magic of that Eternal Moulder by whose infinite power a million suns are shapen more readily than one small jar might be rounded upon my wheel?"

Yet the command of the Celestial and August might never be disobeyed; and the patient workman strove with all his power to fulfil the Son of Heaven's desire. But vainly for days, for weeks, for months, for season after season, did he strive; vainly also he prayed unto the gods to aid him; vainly he besought the Spirit of the Furnace, crying: "O thou Spirit of Fire, hear me, heed me, help me! how shall I,—a miserable man, unable to breathe into clay a living soul,—how shall I render in this inanimate substance the aspect of flesh made to creep by the utterance of a Word, sentient to the horripilation of a Thought?"

For the Spirit of the Furnace made strange answer to him with whispering of fire: "*Vast thy faith, weird thy prayer! Has Thought feet, that man may perceive the trace of its passing? Canst thou measure me the blast of the Wind?*"

Nevertheless, with purpose unmoved, nine-and-forty times did Pu seek to fulfil the Emperor's command; nine-and-forty times he strove to obey the behest of the Son of Heaven. Vainly, alas! did he consume his substance; vainly did he expend his strength; vainly did he exhaust his knowledge: success smiled not upon him; and Evil visited his home, and Poverty sat in his dwelling, and Misery shivered at his hearth.

Sometimes, when the hour of trial came, it was found that the colors had become strangely transmuted in the firing, or had faded into ashen pallor, or had darkened into the fuliginous hue of forest-mould. And Pu, beholding these misfortunes, made wail to the Spirit of the Furnace, praying: "O thou Spirit of Fire, how shall I render the likeness of lustrous flesh, the warm glow of living color, unless thou aid me?"

And the Spirit of the Furnace mysteriously answered him with murmuring of fire: "*Canst thou learn the art of that Infinite Enameller who hath made beautiful the Arch of Heaven,—whose brush is Light; whose paints are the Colors of the Evening?*"

Sometimes, again, even when the tints had not changed, after the pricked and labored surface had seemed about to quicken in the heat, to assume the vibratility of living skin,—even at the last hour all the labor of the workers proved to have been wasted; for the fickle substance rebelled against their efforts, producing only crinklings grotesque as those upon the rind of a withered fruit, or granulations like those upon the skin of a dead bird from which the feathers have been rudely plucked. And Pu wept, and cried out unto the Spirit of the Furnace: "O thou Spirit of Flame, how shall I be able to imitate the thrill of flesh touched by a Thought, unless thou wilt vouchsafe to lend me thine aid?"

And the Spirit of the Furnace mysteriously answered him with muttering of fire: "*Canst thou give ghost unto a stone? Canst thou thrill with a Thought the entrails of the granite hills?*"

Sometimes it was found that all the work indeed had not failed; for the color seemed good, and all faultless the matter of the vase appeared to be, having neither crack nor wrinkling nor crinkling; but the pliant softness of warm skin did not meet the eye; the flesh-tinted surface offered only the harsh aspect and hard glimmer of metal. All their exquisite toil to mock the pulpiness of sentient substance had left no trace; had been brought to nought by the breath of the furnace. And Pu, in his despair, shrieked to the Spirit of the Furnace: "O thou merciless divinity! O thou most pitiless god!—thou whom I have worshipped with ten thousand sacrifices!—for what fault hast thou abandoned me? for what error hast thou forsaken me? How may I, most wretched of men! ever render the aspect of flesh made to creep with the utterance of a Word, sentient to the titillation of a Thought, if thou wilt not aid me?"

And the Spirit of the Furnace made answer unto him with roaring of fire: *"Canst thou divide a Soul? Nay! . . . Thy life for the life of thy work!—thy soul for the soul of thy Vase!"*

And hearing these words Pu arose with a terrible resolve swelling at his heart, and made ready for the last and fiftieth time to fashion his work for the oven.

One hundred times did he sift the clay and the quartz, the *kao-ling* and the *tun;* one hundred times did he purify them in clearest water; one hundred times with tireless hands did he knead the creamy paste, mingling it at last with colors known only to himself. Then was the vase shapen and reshapen, and touched and retouched by the hands of Pu, until its blandness seemed to live, until it appeared to quiver and to palpitate, as with vitality from within, as with the quiver of rounded muscle undulating beneath the integument. For the hues of life were upon it and infiltrated throughout its innermost substance, imitating the carnation of blood-bright tissue, and the reticulated purple of the veins; and over all was laid the envelope of sun-colored *Pe-kia-ho*, the lucid and glossy enamel, half diaphanous, even like the substance that it counterfeited,—the polished skin of a woman. Never since the making of the world had any work comparable to this been wrought by the skill of man.

Then Pu bade those who aided him that they should feed the furnace well with wood of *tcha;* but he told his resolve unto none. Yet after the oven began to glow, and he saw the work of his hands blossoming and blushing in the heat, he bowed himself before the Spirit of Flame, and murmured: "O thou Spirit and Master of Fire, I know the truth of thy words! I know that a Soul may never be divided! Therefore my life for the life of my work!—my soul for the soul of my Vase!"

And for nine days and for eight nights the furnaces were fed unceasingly with wood of *tcha;* for nine days and for eight nights men watched the wondrous vase crystallizing into being, rose-lighted by the breath of the flame. Now upon the coming of the ninth night, Pu bade all his weary comrades retire to rest, for that the work was well-nigh done, and the success assured. "If you find me not here at sunrise," he said, "fear not to take forth the vase; for I know that the task will have been accomplished according to the command of the August." So they departed.

But in that same ninth night Pu entered the flame, and yielded up his ghost in the embrace of the Spirit of the Furnace, giving his life for the life of his work,— his soul for the soul of his Vase.

And when the workmen came upon the tenth morning to take forth the porcelain marvel, even the bones of Pu had ceased to be; but lo! the Vase lived as they looked upon it: seeming to be flesh moved by the utterance of a Word, creeping to the titillation of a Thought. And whenever tapped by the finger it uttered a voice and a name,—the voice of its maker, the name of its creator: PU.

And the son of Heaven, hearing of these things, and viewing the miracle of the vase, said unto those about him: "Verily, the Impossible hath been wrought by the strength of faith, by the force of obedience! Yet never was it our desire that so cruel a sacrifice should have been; we sought only to know whether the skill of the matchless artificer came from the Divinities or from the Demons,—from heaven or from hell. Now, indeed, we discern that Pu hath taken his place among the gods." And the Emperor mourned exceedingly for his faithful servant. But he ordained that godlike honors should be paid unto the spirit of the marvellous artist, and that his memory should be revered forevermore, and that fair statues of him should be set up in all the cities of the Celestial Empire, and above all the toiling of the potteries, that the multitude of workers might unceasingly call upon his name and invoke his benediction upon their labors.

Notes

"The Soul of the Great Bell."—The story of Ko-Ngai is one of the collection entitled *Pe-Hiao-Tou-Choue,* or "A Hundred Examples of Filial Piety." It is very simply told by the Chinese narrator. The scholarly French consul, P. Dabry de Thiersant, translated and published in 1877 a portion of the book, including the legend of the Bell. His translation is enriched with a number of Chinese drawings; and there is a quaint little picture of Ko-Ngai leaping into the molten metal.

"The Story of Ming-Y."—The singular phantom-tale upon which my work is based forms the thirty-fourth story of the famous collection *Kin-Kou-Ki-Koan,* and was first translated under the title, "La Bachelière du Pays de Chu," by the learned Gustave Schlegel, as an introduction to his publication (accompanied by a French version) of the curious and obscene *Mai-yu-lang-toú-tchen-hoa-koueï* (Leyden, 1877), which itself forms the seventh recital of the same work. Schlegel, Julien, Gardner, Birch, D'Entrecolles, Rémusat, Pavie, Olyphant, Grisebach, Hervey-Saint-Denys, and others, have given the Occidental world translations of eighteen stories from the *Kin-Kou-Ki-Koan;* namely, Nos. 2, 3, 5, 6, 7, 8, 10, 14, 19, 20, 26, 27, 29, 30, 31, 34, 35, and 39. The Chinese work itself dates back to the thirteenth century; but as it forms only a collection of the most popular tales of that epoch, many of the stories selected by the Chinese editor may have had a much more ancient origin. There are forty tales in the *Kin-Kou-Ki-Koan.*

"The Legend of Tchi-Niu."—My authority for this tale is the following legend from the thirty-fourth chapter of the *Kan-ing-p'ien,* or "Book of Rewards and Punishments,"—a work attributed to Lao-tseu, which contains some four hundred anecdotes and traditions of the most curious kind:—

> Tong-yong, who lived under the Han dynasty, was reduced to a state of extreme poverty. Having lost his father, he sold himself in order to obtain . . . the where-withal to bury him and to build him a tomb. The Master of Heaven took pity on him, and sent the Goddess Tchi-Niu to him to become his wife. She wove a piece of silk for him every day until she was able to buy his freedom, after which she gave him a son, and went back to heaven.—*Julien's French Translation,* p. 119.

Lest the reader should suppose, however, that I have drawn wholly upon my own imagination for the details of the apparition, the cure, the marriage ceremony, etc., I refer him to No. XCVI. of Giles's "Strange Stories from a Chinese Studio," entitled, "A Supernatural Wife," in which he will find that my narrative is at least conformable to Chinese ideas. (This story first appeared in "Harper's Bazar," and is republished here by permission.)

"The Return of Yen-Tchin-King."—There may be an involuntary anachronism in my version of this legend, which is very pithily narrated in the *Kan-ing-p'ien.* No emperor's name is cited by the homilist; and the date of the revolt seems to have been left wholly to conjecture.— Baber, in his "Memoirs," mentions one of his Mongol archers as able to bend a two-hundred-pound bow until the ears met.

"The Tradition of the Tea-Plant."—My authority for this bit of folklore is the brief statement published by Bretschneider in the "Chinese Recorder" for 1871:—

> "A Japanese legend says that about A.D. 519, a Buddhist

priest came to China, and, in order to dedicate his soul entirely to God, he made a vow to pass the day and night in an uninterrupted and unbroken meditation. After many years of this continual watching, he was at length so tired that he fell asleep. On awaking the following morning, he was so sorry he had broken his vow that he cut off both his eyelids and threw them upon the ground. Returning to the same place the following day he observed that each eyelid had become a shrub. This was the *tea-shrub,* unknown until that time."

Bretschneider adds that the legend in question seems not to be known to the Chinese; yet in view of the fact that Buddhism itself, with all its marvellous legends, was received by the Japanese from China, it is certainly probable this legend had a Chinese origin,—subsequently disguised by Japanese chronology. My Buddhist texts were drawn from Fernand Hû's translation of the Dhammapada, and from Leon Feer's translation from the Thibetan of the "Sutra in Forty-two Articles." An Orientalist who should condescend in a rare leisure-moment to glance at my work might also discover that I had borrowed an idea or two from the Sanscrit poet, Bhâminî-Vilâsa.

"The Tale of the Porcelain-God."—The good Père d'Entrecolles, who first gave to Europe the secrets of Chinese porcelain-manufacture, wrote one hundred and sixty years ago:—

"The Emperors of China are, during their lifetime, the most redoubted of divinities; and they believe that nothing should ever stand in the way of their desires. . . .

"It is related that once upon a time a certain Emperor insisted that some porcelains should be made for him according to a model which he gave. It was answered that the thing was simply impossible; but all such remonstrances only served to excite his desire more and more. . . . The officers charged by the demigod to supervise and hasten the work treated the workmen with great harshness. The poor wretches spent all their money, took exceeding pains, and received only blows in return. One of them, in a fit of despair, leaped into the blazing furnace, and was instantly burnt to ashes. But the porcelain that was being baked there at the time came out, they say, perfectly beautiful and to the satisfaction of the Emperor. . . . From that time, the unfortunate workman was regarded as a hero; and his image was made the idol which presides over the manufacture of porcelain."

It appears that D'Entrecolles mistook the statue of Pou't'ai, God of Comfort, for that of the real porcelain-deity, as Jacquemart and others observe. This error does not, however, destroy the beauty of the myth; and there is no good reason to doubt that D'Entrecolles related it as it had been told him by some of his Chinese friends at King-te-chin. The researches of Stanislas Julien and others have only tended to confirm the trustworthiness of the Catholic missionary's statements in other respects; and both Julien and Salvétat, in their admirable French rendering of the *King-te-chin-thao-lou,* "History of the Porcelains of King-te-chin" (a work which has been of the greatest service to me in the preparation of my little story), quote from his letters at considerable length, and award him the highest praise as a conscientious investigator. So far as I have been able to learn, D'Entrecolles remains the sole authority for the myth; but his affirmations in regard to other matters have withstood the severe tests of time astonishingly well; and since the Tai-ping rebellion destroyed King-te-chin and paralyzed its noble industry, the value of the French missionary's documents and testimony has become widely recognized. In lieu of any other name for the hero of the legend, I have been obliged to retain that of Pou, or Pu,—

 only using it without the affix "t'ai,"—so as to distinguish it from the deity of comfort and repose.

Glossary

ABHIDHARMA—The metaphysics of Buddhism. Buddhist literature is classed into three great divisions, or "baskets"; the highest of these is the Abhidharma. . . . According to a passage in Spence Hardy's "Manual of Buddhism," the full comprehension of the Abhidharma is possible only for a Buddha to acquire.

CHIH—"House"; but especially the house of the dead,— a tomb.

CHU-SHA-KIH—The mandarin-orange.

ÇRAMANA—An ascetic; one who has subdued his senses. For an interesting history of this term, see Burnouf,— "Introduction à l'histoire du Buddhisme Indien."

DAMÂRI—A peculiar chant, of somewhat licentious character, most commonly sung during the period of the Indian carnival. For an account, at once brief and entertaining, of Hindoo popular songs and hymns, see Garcin de Tassy,— "Chants populaires de l'Inde."

DOGS OF FO—The *Dog of Fo* is one of those fabulous monsters in the sculptural representation of which Chinese art has found its most grotesque expression. It is really an exaggerated lion; and the symbolical relation of the lion to Buddhism is well known. Statues of these mythical animals—sometimes of a grandiose and colossal execution— are placed in pairs before the entrances of temples, palaces, and tombs, as tokens of honor, and as emblems of divine protection.

79

FO—Buddha is called *Fo, Fuh, Fuh-tu, Hwut, Făt,* in various Chinese dialects. The name is thought to be a corruption of the Hindoo *Bodh,* or "Truth," due to the imperfect articulation of the Chinese. . . . It is a curious fact that the Chinese Buddhist liturgy is Sanscrit transliterated into Chinese characters, and that the priests have lost all recollection of the antique tongue,—repeating the texts without the least comprehension of their meaning.

FUH-YIN—An official holding in Chinese cities a position corresponding to that of mayor in the Occident.

FUNG-HOANG—This allegorical bird, corresponding to the Arabian phœnix in some respects, is described as being five cubits high, having feathers of five different colors, and singing in five modulations. . . . The female is said to sing in imperfect tones; the male in perfect tones. The *fung-hoang* figures largely in Chinese musical myths and legends.

GOPIA (*or* GOPÎS)—Daughters and wives of the cowherds of Vrindavana, among whom Krishna was brought up after his incarnation as the eighth avatar of Vishnu. Krishna's amours with the shepherdesses, or Gopia, form the subject of various celebrated mystical writings, especially the *Prem-Ságar,* or "Ocean of Love" (translated by Eastwick and by others); and the sensuous *Gita-Govinda* of the Bengalese lyric poet Jayadeva (translated into French prose by Hippolyte Fauche, and chastely rendered into English verse by Edwin Arnold in the "Indian Song of Songs"). See also Burnouf's partial translation of the *Bhagavata Purana,* and Théodore Pavie's "Kriçhna et sa doctrine." . . . The same theme has inspired some of the strangest productions of Hindoo art: for examples, see plates 65 and 66 of Moor's "Hindoo Pantheon" (edition of 1861). For accounts of the erotic mysticism connected with the worship of Krishna and the Gopia, the reader may also be referred to authorities cited in Barth's "Religions of India"; De Tassy's "Chants populaires de l'Inde"; and Lamairesse's "Poésies populaires du Sud de l'Inde."

HAO-KHIEOU-TCHOUAN—This celebrated Chinese novel was translated into French by M. Guillard d'Arcy in 1842, and appeared under the title, "Hao-Khieou-Tchouan; ou, La Femme Accomplie." The first translation of the romance into any European tongue was a Portuguese rendering; and the English version of Percy is based upon the Portuguese text. The work is rich in poetical quotations.

HEÏ-SONG-CHÉ-TCHOO—"One day when the Emperor Hiuan-tsong of the Thang dynasty," says the *Tao-kia-ping-yu-che*, "was at work in his study, a tiny Taoist priest, no bigger than a fly, rose out of the inkstand lying upon his table, and said to him: 'I am the Genius of ink; my name is Heï-song-ché-tchoo [*Envoy of the Black Fir*]; and I have come to tell you that whenever a true sage shall sit down to write, the Twelve Divinities of Ink [*Long-pinn*] will appear upon the surface of the ink he uses.'" See "L'Encre de Chine," by Maurice Jametel. Paris, 1882.

HOA-TCHAO—The "Birthday of a Hundred Flowers" falls upon the fifteenth of the second spring-moon.

JADE—Jade, or nephrite, a variety of jasper,—called by the Chinese *yuh*,—has always been highly valued by them as artistic material. . . . In the "Book of Rewards and Punishments," there is a curious legend to the effect that Confucius, after the completion of his *Hiao-King* ("Book of Filial Piety"), having addressed himself to Heaven, a crimson rainbow fell from the sky, and changed itself at his feet into a piece of yellow jade. See Stanislas Julien's translation, p. 495.

KABIT—A poetical form much in favor with composers of Hindoo religious chants: the *kabit* always consists of four verses.

KAO-LING—Literally, "the High Ridge," and originally the name of a hilly range which furnished the best quality of clay to the porcelain-makers. Subsequently the term applied by long custom to designate the material itself became corrupted into the word now familiar in all countries,—kaolin. In the language of the Chinese potters, the *kaolin,* or clay, was poetically termed the "bones," and the *tun,* or quartz, the "flesh" of the porcelain; while the prepared bricks of the combined substances were known as *pe-tun-tse.* Both substances, the infusible and the fusible, are productions of the same geological formation,—decomposed feldspathic rock.

KASÍ (*or* VARANASI)—Ancient name of Benares, the "Sacred City," believed to have been founded by the gods. It is also called "The Lotos of the World." Barth terms it "the Jerusalem of all the sects both of ancient and modern India." It still boasts two thousand shrines, and half a million images of divinities. See also Sherring's "Sacred City of the Hindoos."

KIANG-KOU-JIN—Literally, the "tell-old-story-men." For a brief account of Chinese professional story-tellers, the reader may consult Schlegel's entertaining introduction to the *Mai-yu-lang-toú-tchen-hoa-koueï.*

KIN—The most perfect of Chinese musical instruments, also called "the Scholar's Lute." The word *kin* also means "to prohibit"; and this name is said to have been given to the instrument because music, according to Chinese belief, *"restrains evil passions, and corrects the human heart."* See Williams's "Middle Kingdom."

KOUEI—Kouei, musician to the Emperor Yao, must have held his office between 2357 and 2277 B.C. The extract selected from one of his songs, which I have given at the beginning of the "Story of Ming-Y," is therefore more than four thousand years old. The same chant contains another remarkable fancy, evidencing Chinese faith in musical magic:—

> "When I smite my [*musical*] stone,—
> Be it gently, be it strongly,—
> Then do the fiercest beasts of prey leap high for joy,
> And the chiefs among the public officials do agree among
>   themselves."

KWANG-CHAU-FU—Literally, "The Broad City,"—the name of Canton. It is also called "The City of Genii."

LÍ—A measure of distance. The length of the *lí* has varied considerably in ancient and in modern times. The present is given by Williams as ten *lí* to a league.

LI-SAO—"The Dissipation of Grief," one of the most celebrated Chinese poems of the classic period. It is said to have been written about 314 B.C., by Kiu-ping-youen, minister to the King of Tsou. Finding himself the victim of a base court-intrigue, Kiu-ping wrote the *Li-Sao* as a vindication of his character, and as a rebuke to the malice of his enemies, after which he committed suicide by drowning. . . . A fine French translation of the *Li-Sao* has been made by the Marquis Hervey de Saint-Denys (Paris, 1870).

LI-SHU—The second of the six styles of Chinese writing, for an account of which see Williams's "Middle Kingdom." . . . According to various Taoist legends, the decrees of Heaven are recorded in the "Seal-character," the oldest of all; and marks upon the bodies of persons killed by lightning have been interpreted as judgments written in it. The following extraordinary tale from the *Kan-ing-p'ien* affords a good example of the superstition in question:—

> Tchang-tchun was Minister of State under the reign of Hoeï-tsong, of the Song dynasty. He occupied himself wholly in weaving perfidious plots. He died in exile at Mo-tcheou. Sometime after, while the Emperor was hunting, there fell a heavy rain, which obliged him to seek shelter in a poor man's hut. The thunder rolled with violence; and the lightning killed a man, a woman, and a little boy. On the backs of the man and woman were found red characters, which could not be deciphered; but on the back of the little boy the following six words could be read, written in Tchouen (*antique*) characters: TSÉ-TCH'IN-TCHANG-TCHUN-HEOU-CHIN,—which mean: "Child of the issue of Tchang-tchun, who was a rebellious subject."—*Le Livre des Récompenses et des Peines, traduit par Stanislas Julien*, p. 446.

PAGAL—The ankle-ring commonly worn by Hindoo women; it is also called *nupur*. It is hollow, and contains loose bits of metal, which tinkle when the foot is moved.

SAN-HIEN—A three-stringed Chinese guitar. Its belly is usually covered with snake-skin.

SIU-FAN-TI—Literally, "the Sweeping of the Tombs,"— the day of the general worship of ancestors; the Chinese "All-Souls'." It falls in the early part of April, the period called *tsing-ming*.

TA-CHUNG SZ'—Literally, "Temple of the Bell." The building at Pekin so named covers probably the largest suspended bell in the world, cast in the reign of Yong-lo, about 1406 A.D., and weighing upwards of 120,000 pounds.

TAO—The infinite being, or Universal Life, whence all forms proceed: Literally, "the Way," in the sense of the First Cause. Lao-tseu uses the term in other ways; but that primal and most important philosophical sense which he gave to it is well explained in the celebrated Chapter XXV. of the *Tao-te-king*. . . . The difference between the great Chinese thinker's conception of the First Cause—the Unknowable,—and the theories of other famous metaphysicians, Oriental and Occidental, is set forth with some definiteness in Stanislas Julien's introduction to the *Tao-te-king*, pp. x-xv. ("Le Livre de la Voie et de la Vertu." Paris, 1842.)

THANG—The Dynasty of Thang, which flourished between 620 and 907 A.D., encouraged literature and art, and gave to China its most brilliant period. The three poets of the Thang dynasty mentioned in the second story flourished between 779 and 852 A.D.

"THREE COUNCILLORS."—Six stars of the Great-Bear constellation ($\iota\kappa$—$\lambda\mu$—$\nu\xi$), as apparently arranged in pairs, are thus called by the Chinese astrologers and mythologists. The three couples are further distinguished as the Superior Councillor, Middle Councillor, and Inferior

Councillor; and, together with the Genius of the Northern Heaven, form a celestial tribunal, presiding over the duration of human life, and deciding the course of mortal destiny. (Note by Stanislas Julien in "Le Livre des Récompenses et des Peines.")

TIEN-HIA—Literally, "Under-Heaven," or "Beneath-the-Sky,"—one of the most ancient of those many names given by the Chinese to China. The name "China" itself is never applied by the Black-haired Race to their own country, and is supposed to have had its origin in the fame of the first *Tsin* dynasty, whose founder, Tsin Chí-Houang-tí, built the Great, or "Myriad-Mile," Wall, twenty-two and a half degrees of latitude in length. . . . See Williams regarding occurrence of the name "China" in Sanscrit literature.

TSIEN—The well-known Chinese copper coin, with a square hole in the middle for stringing, is thus named. According to quality of metal it takes from 900 to 1,800 *tsien* to make one silver dollar.

TSING-JIN—"Men of Tsing." From very ancient times the Chinese have been wont to call themselves by the names of their famous dynasties,—*Han-jin,* "the men of Han"; *Thang-jin,* "the men of Thang," etc. *Ta Tsing Kwoh* ("Great Pure Kingdom") is the name given by the present dynasty to China,—according to which the people might call themselves *Tsing-jin,* or "men of Tsing." Williams, however, remarks that they will not yet accept the appellation.

VERSES (CHINESE)—The verses preceding "The Legend of Tchi-Niu" afford some remarkable examples of Chinese onomatopœia. They occur in the sixth strophe of *Miên-miên,* which is the third chant of the first section of *Ta-ya,* the Third Book of the *Chi-King.* (See G. Pauthier's French version.) Dr. Legge translates the strophe thus:—

> . . . Crowds brought the earth in baskets; they threw it with shouts into the frames; they beat it with responsive blows; they pared the walls repeatedly till they sounded

strong—*Sacred Books of the East;* Vol. III., *The She-King*, p. 384.

Pauthier translates the verses somewhat differently; preserving the onomatopœia in three of the lines. *Hoûng-hoûng* are the sounds heard in the timber-yards where the wood is being measured; from the workshops of the builders respond the sounds of *tông-tông;* and the solid walls, when fully finished off, give out the sound of *pîng-pîng.*

YAO—"Porcelain." The reader who desires detailed information respecting the technology, history, or legends of Chinese porcelain-manufacture should consult Stanislas Julien's admirable "Histoire de la Porcelaine Chinoise" (Paris, 1856). With some trifling exceptions, the names of the various porcelains cited in my "Tale of the Porcelain-God" were selected from Julien's work. Though oddly musical and otherwise attractive in Chinese, these names lose interest by translation. The majority of them merely refer to centres of manufacture or famous potteries: *Chou-yao,* "porcelains of Chou"; *Hong-tcheou-yao,* "porcelains of Hong-tcheou"; *Jou-yao,* "porcelains of Jou-tcheou"; *Ting-yao,* "porcelains of Ting-tcheou"; *Ko-yao,"* porcelains of the Elder Brother [Thsang]"; *Khang-hi-nien-t'sang-yao,* "porcelains of Thsang made in the reign of Khang-hi." Some porcelains were distinguished by the names of dynasties, or the titles of civic office holders; such as the celebrated *Tch'aï-yao,* "the porcelains of Tch'aï" (which was the name of the family of the Emperor Chi-tsong); and the *Kouan-yao,* or "Porcelains of Magistrates." Much more rarely the names refer directly to the material or artistic peculiarity of porcelains,—as *Ou-ni-yao,* the "black-paste porcelains," or *Pi-se-yao,* the "porcelains of hidden color."

The word *khi,* sometimes substituted for *yao* in these compound names, means "vases"; as *Jou-khi,* "vases of Jou-tcheou"; *Kouan-khi,* "vases for Magistrates."